WELLINGTON

in action

By Ron Mackay
Color by Don Greer
Illustrated by Joe Sewell

Aircraft Number 76

squadron/signal publications, inc.

Wellington Mk IC of No 214 Squadron flown by Pilot/Officer Geoff Cole returning to RAF Standishall after a mission to Germany during 1940.

Royal Air Force
Bomber Command

ISBN 0-89747-183-0

If you have any photographs of the aircraft, armor, soldiers or ships of any nation, particularly wartime snapshots, why not share them with us and help make Squadron/Signal's books all the more interesting and complete in the future. Any photograph sent to us will be copied and the original returned. The donor will be fully credited for any photos used. Please send them to: Squadron/Signal Publications Inc. 1115 Crowley Dr., Carrollton, TX 75011-5010.

DEDICATION

This book is sincerely dedicated to all Wellington men, be they aircrew or ground crew, with a special reference to my good friend Jack Wade and to the late Seymour 'Barney' Barnard.

CONTRIBUTORS

BRUCE ROBERTSON	JOHN D R RAWLINGS
RICHARD LEASK WARD	JERRY C SCUTTS
REG PANNELL	NORMAL DIDWELL
RON LIVERSAGE	HUGH MANSELL
T H CLARIDGE	L G GREGORY
S STOCKFORD	GEOFF COLE
JACK WADE	BERNARD BAINES
STAN BISHOP	MRS G PRITCHARD
JACK ROGERS	IMPERIAL WAR MUSEUM
RAF MUSEUM	CANADIAN ARMED FORCES
HANS ROSSBACH	

Special thanks is also due Colin Francis and Peter Pallett who provided an immeasurable degree of service in producing so much of the photographic content of this book.

With the sun setting behind them an aircrew climbs aboard their Wellington Mk 1C, a scene that was to be repeated countless times as darkness fell during the next four years.

INTRODUCTION

Sadly, of the many thousands of British bombers constructed during World War II only a handful still exist. Consequently visitors to the Royal Air Force Museum in London are privileged to view the sole intact example of the Vickers Wellington medium bomber, which is especially ironic in view of the numbers produced, and the Wellington's comprehensive use by the Royal Air Force.

Built in appreciatively greater numbers than any of its Bomber Command contemporaries, the Wellington served on all major battle fronts, and in a great variety of roles. While its primary function was that of a bomber its role was extended to the equally important missions of anti-submarine warfare, transport, operational training, and engine experimentation.

Known as the *Cloth Bomber*, its fabric-covered *geodetic* structure combined strength with lightness and flexibility — indeed the quality of flexibility was literally visible, and it became a favorite pastime of experienced crew members to invite passengers or raw aircrew to sit on the main-spar and watch their reaction when the central-support spar fluctuated during the aircraft's start-up and take-off! A standard joke was centered around the airframe's exact dimensions, which it was claimed could never be determined due to the airframe's *flexibility*.

The Wellington's unique geodetic construction was the brainchild of Barnes Wallis, the Vickers designer that would later be responsible for developing the 'Dambuster' mine, as well as the 'Tallboy' and 'Grand Slam' aerodynamic bombs. Geodetic construction, developed and applied to aircraft by Wallis shortly after he joined Vickers Aircraft was a 'basket weave' construction system producing a criss-cross pattern of self stabilizing framework members in which loads in any direction were automatically equalized by forces in the intersecting set of frames, producing high strength at low weight. Geodetic construction was first used in the construction of the Vickers Wellesley, a single-engined bomber which was developed as a private venture by Vickers. The Wellesley prototype (K7556) flew for the first time on 19 June 1935, with orders eventually totaling 174 machines.

The success of the Wellesley gave Vickers the necessary encouragement to submit a design proposal for a geodetic construction all-metal twin-engined bomber in response to the Air Ministry's Specification B9/32 issued in mid-1932 for a day bomber. The Vickers proposal was for a high-winged bomber with a fixed-undercarriage with power being provided by either a pair of 660 hp Bristol Mercury VIs or Rolls Royce Goshawk steam-cooled engines. This airframe/engine combination was deemed more than sufficient to accommodate the B9/32 requirements of hauling a 1,000 pound bomb load over a range of 720 miles. However, after studying the Vickers design the Air Ministry issued greatly revised specifications in September of 1933 superseding the original specifications. The Vickers response to these revised specifications was a geodetic constructioned mid-wing monoplane powered by a pair of Goshawk I engines which were the specified powerplants. The fixed undercarriage specification was supplanted by retractable units which would greatly improve maximum speed.

In December of 1933 Vickers was awarded a contract for the construction of a single prototype under the designation Type 271. Both nose and tail featured rounded framed clear plexiglass gun positions. The cockpit shape and the vertical fin configuration were based on the earlier Stranraer Flying Boat. The rearward and upward swinging fully retractable undercarriage were mounted in the lower engine nacelles just behind the leading edge of the wings, with front-hinged nacelle doors. The fixed tail wheel was enclosed in a teardrop shaped fairing.

The geodetic diamond-shaped pattern had such inherent strength that the use of linear straight metal strip supports was kept to a bare minimum: for example the prototype only bore four lengths along the fuselage, top, bottom, and both sides. During tests carried out earlier on the Wellesley it had been found that the reduction in weight was a full third while the increase in flexure and torsion strength was almost one-hundred percent.

Geodetic Structure

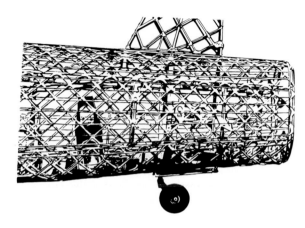

(Below) The sleek cigar shape of the prototype bears little resemblance to what would become the robust and distinctly stocky shape of the production Wellington. The fixed tail wheel has had an aerodynamic fairing added. Color is overall Silver paint with polished metal engine cowlings.

By the time construction had begun the Air Ministry realized that the steam cooled Goshawk I engine was not fulfilling its early promise and the specifications were again changed, this time to include an alternative powerplant. The more powerful, but heavier 850 hp Bristol Pegasus nine cylinder air cooled radial engine was installed.

On 15 June 1936 Vickers Chief Test pilot J 'Mutt' Summers flew the prototype (K4049) for the first time from the Vickers main production plant, located in the center of the famous Brooklands racing track southwest of London at Weybridge. The new bomber was capable of lifting a bomb load of 4,500 pounds and had a range of 2,800 miles — quadrupling both of these performance aspects when set against the original specifications.

The tentative choice of name accorded to the new bomber was *Crécy*, taken from a French city, which was strange in view of the Air Ministry's general policy of using British town names for multi-engined aircraft. However, within two months a change was made to the much more fitting name of **Wellington**, and at about the same time the RAF placed its initial order for 180 aircraft. In addition, the Air Ministry again altered the basic specifications under the terms of B29/36 in February of 1937. The aircraft was now expected to conform to the requirements for a *medium night bomber* — even though the RAF was currently a day bombing force and was to enter World War II with its policy still firmly wedded to the concept of daylight operations.

Among the features introduced under these revised specifications was the addition of power operated gun turrets of Vickers design using hydraulically operated controls of Frazer Nash origin. Three turrets were mooted, for the nose, tail and ventral positions, with the ventral turret being fully retractable. In addition a manually operated dorsal gun was to be mounted and fired through a sliding hatch above the central fuselage area. Although only the tail turret bore twin gun fittings, the principle of powered turrets was an advanced concept for the Mid-1930s. It is one of the ironic twists in aviation history that whereas Britain lagged behind in features such as navigation and blind-bombing aids, self-sealing tanks and armored protection, she was in the forefront of power operated turret development when the War began. However, this superiority was to be somewhat eroded by the dependence on .303 caliber machine guns as opposed to larger rifle calibers, such as the .50 caliber, or cannons.

The prototype of the Wellington, however, was fated not to be modified to the new specifications. On 19 April 1937, while flying out of the Aircraft and Armament Establishment at Martlesham Heath on one of its last trial flights the aircraft suffered a fatal accident when it broke up during an involuntary high-speed dive.

Elevator imbalance was determined as the cause of the prototype's crash. To correct the problem a revised fin, rudder and elevator was adapted from the parallel Vickers B1/35 development aircraft which would enter service in 194? as the Warwick. However, it is probable that the prototype would never have been fully modified since modification involved structural modification, especially to the rear fuselage around the vertical fin.

The ill fated K4049 was the first of 11,461 Wellingtons built, with construction continuing into 1945. For the first three years of the War the Wimpy (an affectionate nickname derived from the Popeye cartoon character J Wellington Wimpy) shouldered, in the company of its Hampden and Whitley twin-engined cousins, the burden of carrying out an offensive campaign to the enemy when British forces were nearly everywhere on the defensive. Flying in all kinds of weather with minimal navigation and radar aids to assist them, Wellington crews fought in the face of steadily increasing German defenses and mounting losses. In so doing these pioneers paved the way for the huge night offensive beginning in 1943, which along with the USAAF daylight assaults would last until 1945, and ultimately grind down the enemy's industrial resources as well as his army's ability to resist on the field of battle.

Coastal Command also operated the Wellington both at home and abroad. Bomber Command squadrons flew the Wellington from bases in North Africa, Italy and Burma between 1940 and 1945. Just as the Wellington leads in numbers produced, so it was also the sole Bomber type to see operational service from 1939 to 1945.

(Below) The prototype had generous but flat angular panels in the cockpit. The nose and tail cones have been covered to prevent an on looker from seeing the still secret geodetic fuselage structure. Type A roundels are carried in all six wing and fuselage locations.

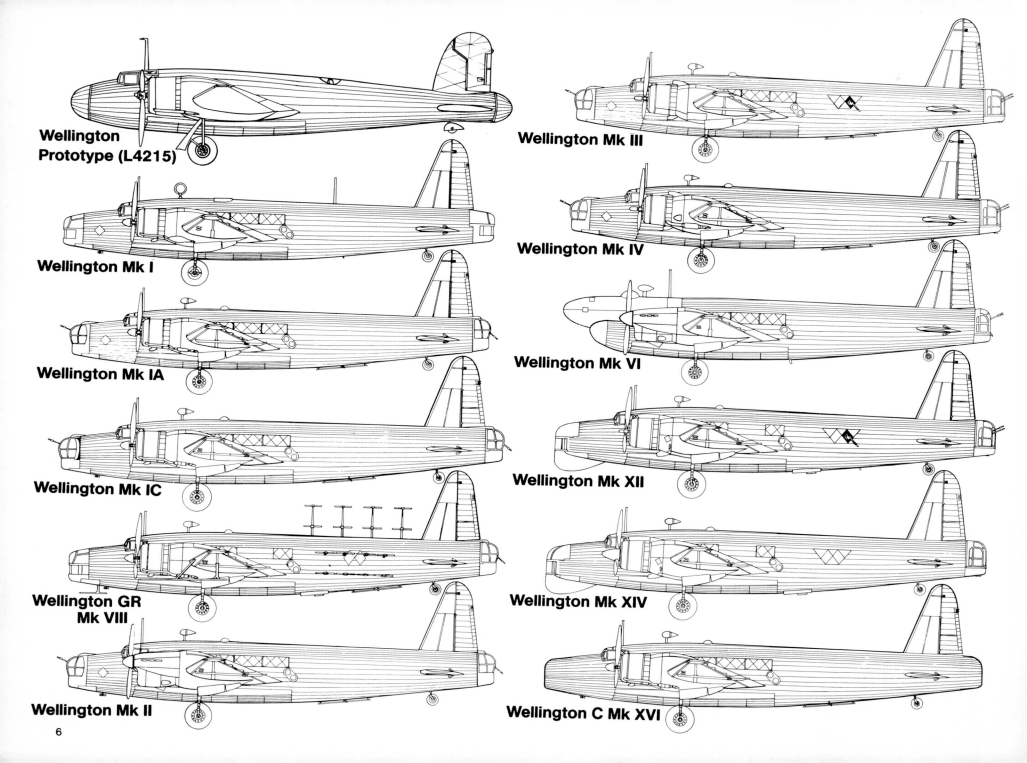

Wellington
Prototype (L4215)

Wellington Mk I

Wellington Mk IA

Wellington Mk IC

Wellington GR
Mk VIII

Wellington Mk II

Wellington Mk III

Wellington Mk IV

Wellington Mk VI

Wellington Mk XII

Wellington Mk XIV

Wellington C Mk XVI

Wellington Mk I

To solve the problem found to be the cause of the prototype crash new tail surfaces were added to L4212, which would serve as the production prototype for the Wellington I. Another change made to L4212 the replacement of the angular flat-panels of the prototype cockpit enclosure for plexi-glass panels which were contoured to the fuselage cross-section, with flat panels on the windscreen which cut down sun glare and reflection that had been reported by the prototype's test pilots. The tail wheel fairing was removed and made fully retractable. L4212 had only two windows on each side of the fuselage while production aircraft carried five windows on each side.

Carrying the new power gun turrets the prototype of the Wellington I flew for the first time on 23 December 1937, powered by Pegasus XX engines in place of the intended Pegasus XVIII engines which had yet to be cleared. The nose heaviness experienced during in test dives was solved by introducing a modified elevator which incorporated horn balances which were installed on L4213 which first flew on 9 September 1938. The operation of the flaps and elevator trim-tabs were linked in a further and successful bid to cure the tail heaviness condition. Cockpit heating and de-icing provisions were made, with both devices being a necessity at the 10 to 15,000 foot altitude which Wellington operations were to be conducted. Another feature brought into service was the use of three-bladed constant-speed propellers produced by De Haviland/Hamilton.

Initially, production was exceedingly slow, with the Weybridge factory being capable of producing only one machine per day. However, before long production lines were laid down at Squires Gate, Blackpool and at Chester. L4215, the first of the eventual 181 Wellington Mk Is to be manufactured, was delivered to No 99 Squadron at Mildenhall, Suffolk on 10 October 1938. By the following September when war broke out, fully eight Squadrons, all under the charge of No 3 Group based in East Anglia, were ready for operations. In addition, No 75 and 148 Squadrons were on Group Reserve Status at RAF Harwell near London. During the preceding eleven months the emphasis in the flying training program had been on close formation flying, it being the confident hope that the bombers' combined gunfire while in close formation would be sufficient to ward off fighter attacks. However, during the first few months of the war this 'confident hope' was to prove not only tragically deficient, but in the 20/20 vision of hindsight ... it was naive.

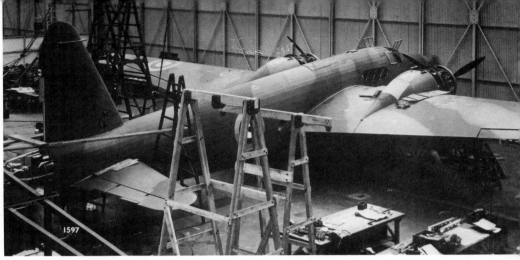

(Above) This Wellington Mk I on the production line is believed to be L4212, the production prototype of the Wellington as is evidenced by the very short fuselage window strip. Later production Mk Is carried fuselage window strips extending to the wing trailing edge.

(Below) The second Wellington Mk I prototype (L4213) does not carry spinner fairings on its propellers which were generally carried on production Mk Is. The distinctive 'bar' link between the wheel hub and the undercarriage leg are on both main wheels. This aircraft never saw operational service, being relegated to ground instructional duties in December of 1940.

(Right) Women assembly line workers apply the fabric covering over the Wellington's geodetic skeleton. The engine baffle plate through which air was directed via its nine apertures onto the cylinder heads was removed on a few Pegasus engines but was largely a distinctive feature of the Pegasus engined Wellington.

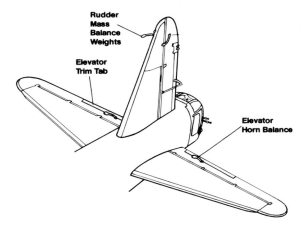

Rudder Mass Balance Weights

Elevator Trim Tab

Elevator Horn Balance

(Below) An early Mk I banks to the starboard over the River Wey during its approach to Weybridge in 1938. The nub silhouetted under the nose is the venturi for the blind-flying instrument panel which was virtually a standard fitting on Wellingtons up to the Mk IC.

Fuselage Windows

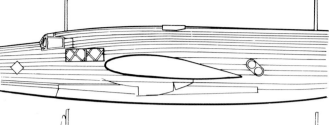

L4212 Production Prototype

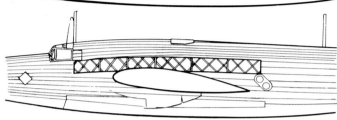

Production Mk I

(Above) L4341 has White crosses painted over the roundels during Air Defense exercises in August of 1939, denoting that it is a 'Westland' aircraft. This machine carries the B camouflage pattern which extends down the fuselage and carries No 214 Squadron code letters which soon changed to BU.

(Below) A line-up of Mk Is at the main Brooklands factory during early 1939. L4225 (at left) was in succession assigned to No 99 Squadron and then No 20 OTU, while L4296 (center) was delivered to No 38 Squadron.

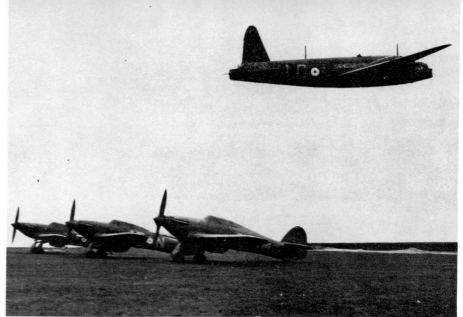

(Above Left) A Mk I of No 148 Squadron during the winter of 1938/39 has the double letters of its call sign stack painted in front of the fuselage roundel. This machine fluctuated between No 148 and No 75 Squadrons followed by OTU service at No 15 and 11's training bases before finally being salvaged in November of 1944.

(Below Left) No 9 Squadron in September of 1939. The distinctive Vickers turret canopies, twin radio masts, and un-faired DF loop were all features of the first operational Wellington. The Double letters used for the aircraft call sign may indicate that Z or A has already been allocated to another bomber. B type fuselage and wing roundels are carried and the Squadron badge can be seen under the cockpit area.

(Above Right) In April of 1940 this No 215 Squadron Mk I Wimpy was borrowed by a No 75 Squadron crew to carry a naval observer from Wick in Northern Scotland on a 2,000 mile round trip to study Kriegsmarine vessel dispositions in the Narvik area of Norway. As it sets out on its Narvik bound flight, the Wellington over-flies three Hurricanes Mk Is.

(Below Right) Crew member on the Narvik — bound Wellington is attending to the flare chute. Immediately behind him is the retracted ventral turret while the circular shape to aircraft's port side is arguabley more important — the Elsan chemical toilet! The semi-circular pads on windows were possibly to aid crew comfort while making observations. The rest bunk can be seen in the right foreground.

10

WELLINGTON MK 1A

The Mark 1A was not a direct line successor to the Mk I, but was rather a design planned in accordance with designing the future Mk II. There were marginal increases in the Mk 1A's dimensions, the fuselage was increased by 6 inches and the wing span was increased by 3 inches. In order to improve the Center of Gravity the aircraft chassis was moved forward three inches.

During trials with the Mk I production prototype the general effectiveness of the Vickers turrets came under critical scrutiny as doubts were raised as to whether the units would be sufficiently effective against the fast fighters in current Luftwaffe service. There was naturally a high degree of opposition from Vickers at the prospect of their equipment being declared redundant without direct evidence of its failure in combat, but the company ultimately bowed to the wishes of RAF authorities and Frazer Nash (FN) turrets were introduced. In contrast to the Vickers turret whose sighting/firing apertures limited the guns' flexibility, the FN5 nose and FN10 tail turrets were completely mobile hydraulic fittings armed with twin .303 machine guns. In the ventral position just behind the bomb-bay an FN9 turret was inserted in a retractable mount.

The exhaust pipe on the starboard engine, which barely extended beyond the rear of the engine cowling, caused problems with flame-streaking during engine start-up which sometimes ignited the fabric under the wing. It was not unusual for groundcrew to hold a bucket over the exhaust orifice while start-up took place! To solve this problem a barbed flame-damper was fitted. By contrast the port engine exhaust pipe had from the first Mk 1 extended back under the wing leading edge. The center section of the port engine exhaust pipe was enclosed in a circular 'muff' which was part of the aircraft's heating system. The first three Mk 1As (N2865, N2866 and N2867) were delivered only hours before war was declared.

Daylight Offensive

The first nine months of the War in Europe on the Western Front, because action on the ground was almost non-existent, became known as the *Phoney War*. However, there was nothing 'Phoney' about the aerial War. Barely twenty-four hours after the British Declaration of War a mixed force of Blenheims and Wellingtons — the latter drawn from the ranks of No 9 and 149 Squadrons — carried out a daylight raid on the German Naval port at Wilhelmshaven. Attacks on land targets were prohibited for fear of creating civilian casualties, hence a concentration on naval targets. The true test for daylight operations still lay some three months in the future, although there were increasingly ominous signs of what lay ahead for Bomber Command. On 29 September five Hampdens were downed off the Friesien Islands when they were intercepted by German fighters, and the Brunsbuttel raid witnessed the loss of two Wellingtons in return for rather ineffective strikes on German ships.

While initial operations were carried out by Wellington Mk 1s, the Mk 1A was coming into large-scale service and would largely supplant the Mk 1 by December of 1939. On 3 December when a *Reconnaissance in Force* was briefed with the Naval base at Heligoland Bight as the target, the Mk I was totally absent, having been replaced by the Wellington Mk 1A. Bombers of No 38, 115 and 149 Squadrons carried out high-level bombing runs, completing their missions without loss, but also with little tangible results. However, eleven days later when a low-level attack by twelve aircraft of 99 Squadron ran into heavy flak as well as fighters, in what was the first air battle of any noticeable scale involving *strategic bombers* in World War II, a large dent was put into the close formation and concentrated firepower theory of defense. Five Wellingtons were shot down with one crashing on the homeward leg. Only one fighter could be claimed against what was a fifty percent loss to Bomber Command.

The ship mooring points at Schillig Roads and Wilhelmshaven were the selected targets for the next Reconnaissance in Force on 18 December with the Wellington force being doubled to twenty four Mk 1As, shared between 9, 37, and 149 Squadrons. Weather conditions were bright and clear as the Wellingtons droned across the North Sea, unaware that an experimental German early warning radar site on Wangerooge Island had picked up and reported their movements. However, lack of experience with the use of radar the RAF aircraft were able to penetrate to the Wilhelmshaven region where after an abortive effort to drop their loads they turned for home without interference from the Luftwaffe. However, units of JG 2 and ZG 76 flying single engine Bf 109s and twin engine Bf 110s had been 'scrambled' and were in a position to intercept the Wellingtons as they were skirting the Friesien Islands on their way home.

(Above) Crewmembers entering their Mk IA bomber. The new Frazer Nash FN5 nose turret fit tightly and overlapped the fuselage when traversed the full ninety degrees. The rear entrance/escape doors are fully exposed when the turret is fully traversed.

The Battle of Heligoland Bight, or The Massacre of Heligoland Bight, depending on one's point of view, was traumatic for Bomber Command, pointing up almost every defect in both equipment and tactics. The limited traverse of the nose gun turrets to less than ninety degrees when combined with the absence of beam weapons permitted the Luftwaffe fighters to attack almost with impunity from above at the midship angle. The fighter's angle of attack often did not permit the Wellington gunners to even sight their adversaries. Even when the gun turrets could be brought to bear on the enemy the superior range and hitting power of the heavier weapons of the German fighters put the bombers at a tremendous disadvantage. Furthermore, the ventral turret of the Wellington slowed it down by almost fifteen mph, just when maximum speed was of paramount importance.

The already perilous situation of the Wellington raiders worsened by the inexplicable breaking up of the formation into separate groups with one group heading due North for some minutes before turning west, trailing the other group which had maintained a continuous course for home. Another factor contributing to the disaster was the absence of armor protection for the crew or fuel tanks causing aircraft to be lost to fierce and uncontrollable fires.

The fleeing Wellingtons were harried nearly halfway across the North Sea, which in its cold and forbidding December condition must have quickly claimed the lives of those crew members who survived their aircraft's impact with the water. Ten Wellingtons were destroyed by direct enemy action, two were ditched because of fuel shortage (due to holed fueled tanks), and three force-landed in England. A total of fifteen Wellington casualties against two Bf 109s. Within days of this disaster the decision was made by Bomber Command to turn from the concept of daylight bombing, and for the next four years their efforts against the Reich would be under the protective cover of darkness.

While the Wellington had received a mauling during its use as a day bomber there was little question that the Vickers design had excellent potential. In May of 1940 when all restrictions on bombing Germany were lifted, Wellington Squadrons were in the vanguard of the night air offensive. A number of technical improvements by then had been made to the Wellington. A navigator's astrodome was fitted above the main-spar, matched by the fairing-in of the DF loop. A fuel jettison system with its discharge pipes located outboard of the engines was installed, and for crew comfort sound proofing was added to the main cabin area.

All of these changes and improvements added considerable weight to the Mk 1A increasing its gross to 28,500 pounds and requiring the installation of larger diameter wheels more able to bear the increased weight. The larger tires now protruded below the engine nacelles. This extra weight also had an adverse effect on top speed. Whereas the Mk I could achieve a maximum speed of 267 mph at 15,000 feet the Mk IA was limited to around 250 mph, although the lowering of the ventral turret did cause much of this reduction in speed. Crew complement at this early stage of the War was six, including two pilots (one of which was usually a novice pilot on his first few 'ops'), a combined navigator/bomb aimer known as an observer, a wireless operator, and two air gunners.

(Right) A trio of Mk IAs over-flying Bassingbourn during the Summer of 1940. Although still carrying No 215 Squadron codes the aircraft by this time had been absorbed into 11 OTU. No 215 Squadron did not recommence operations in its own right until December of 1940.

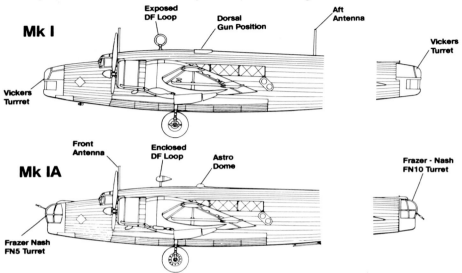

Mk I

Exposed DF Loop
Dorsal Gun Position
Aft Antenna
Vickers Turret
Vickers Turrret

Mk IA

Front Antenna
Enclosed DF Loop
Astro Dome
Frazer - Nash FN10 Turret
Frazer Nash FN5 Turret

(Below) Now on the ground, the trio of Mk 1As seen over-flying Bassingbourn. The fin flash covers the entire vertical fin. The underwing roundels would disappear by late 1940.

Navigation in these early days was by deduced or 'dead reckoning' with the navigator using ground references and, or a sextant with which to navigate by the stars. These navigation methods were adequate so long as the weather was clear, which was not often. With almost unbelievable naivety, at least on the part of the politicians and the Air Ministry, Bomber Command aircraft were dispatched individually to targets and aircrews were allotted specific targets to be bombed within a German city, and dire penalties were threatened on any team which attacked anything but a clearly defined military objective — at least this was the case up to the time when the Luftwaffe began its campaign of bombing cities indiscriminately.

Bomber Command raiders had to traverse up to 350 miles across the North Sea, depending upon the location of the target in enemy territory. Because of this long flight over water the Wellington Mk 1A was fitted with fourteen inflatable flotation bags within the bomb-bay roof which were to be inflated prior to ditching, allowing the Wellington to better withstand the shock of hitting the water and remain afloat, the bomb doors were retained in the closed position. The use of these air bags seems to clearly have been of benefit; a mid-war survey revealed that in a number of specific ditching incidents the crew survival rate was over eighty percent — appreciably higher than other multi-engined aircraft.

WELLINGTON MK IB

The Wellington Mk IB was originally proposed because of problems with the firing of the Vickers gun turrets as well as a Center of Gravity disturbance caused by the ventral turret. There is no record of a Wellington Mk IB variant being produced.

(Right) *A good landing is one you walk away from.* This Mk 1A on its belly is at 20 OTU Lossiemouth in Scotland during 1940. The position of the main wheel and bent propeller blades suggest a collapsed undercarriage during landing or take-off.

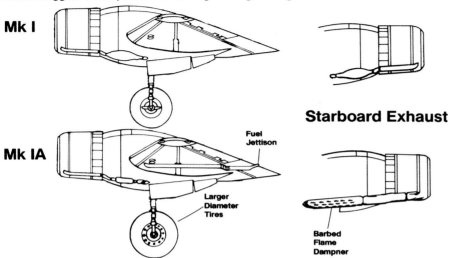

Mk I

Mk IA

Fuel Jettison

Larger Diameter Tires

Starboard Exhaust

Barbed Flame Dampner

(Below Right) Flight Officer Vivien flew Wellington Mk 1C/T2501 to a German target on 4 December 1940, one of two machines out of twelve No 99 Squadron aircraft that got through. Unfortunately the Bomber had to force-land in enemy territory and is seen while under inspection by German military personnel. The aircraft was turned over to the Luftwaff Experimental and Test Center at Rechlin.

Wellington Mk IC

Differing little from the Mk IA, the fuselage of the Wellington Mk IC was slightly cut down behind the nose turret and reshaped in order to allow the nose turret a greater traverse. By contrast the same area on the Mk 1A fit flush with the turret frame. While this modification had the advantage of greater turret mobility it created turbulence when the turret was fully traversed and protruded into the slipstream. Drum-fed Vickers 'K' guns were introduced into beam positions at the midship just ahead of the wing trailing edge, however, after firing trials were carried out with Mk 1A P9211, the Vickers guns were replaced by belt-fed Browning .303 machine guns, with the latter being located further aft. In the event both gun locations were to be seen on both Mk 1As and 1Cs.

Although available records are somewhat vague it appears that the Wellington Mk 1C was the first Wimpy fitted with the Lorenz blind landing beam that featured a horizontal receiving aerial mounted under the rear fuselage slightly to the left of center. While all Mk ICs were not equipped with the Lorenz blind landing equipment, at least a few Mk IAs are believed to have been retro-fitted with the receivers. Internally, a redesigned hydraulic system using VSG pumps was installed along with a twenty-four volt electrical system needed to operate the Directional Radio Compass.

Pegasus XVIII engines were proving to be a generally reliable powerplant, at least when both engines were functioning; however, loss of power in one engine, when combined with a surprising inability to 'feather' the DH propellers, created an all too often inexorable loss of height.

The Wellington Mk 1C was built in much greater quantity than any of the early Pegasus variants with 2,685 aircraft being turned out from all three Vickers plants, with the first delivery being made from Chester on 9 April 1940 direct to No 37 Squadron. By mid-summer the Wellington Mk IC was supplementing the efforts of the Mk 1A over Europe.

From the early summer of 1940, and for the next several years, Bomber Command was the sole indicator to the enslaved peoples of Europe that they had a hope of liberation. However, the first two years of the night offensive starkly outlined Bomber Command's uphill fight to destroy Hitler's Reich with the ordnance and technical devices then at their disposal. The overly optimistic damage reports claiming high levels of destruction to German industry persisted right into late 1941. This optimism was demolished when a number of neutral reports confirmed that bombs were seldom hitting nearer than five miles to the target. The courage, or stubborn perseverance of Bomber Command aircrews was in no way doubted, only the technical means at their disposal to locate a target and accurately deliver their ordnance.

From August of 1941 No 115 Squadron pioneered the operational use of GEE, the first of a trio of navigational and blind-bombing devices whose combined use in early 1943 onwards would eventually revolutionize Bomber Command's nocturnal bombing offensive.

Not only were the bombers having problems in locating and hitting a target, but they were facing an increasingly effective German defensive system. The Kammhuber Line — named after its creator, *Luftwaffe* General Josef Kammhuber — presented Bomber Command with solid bands of searchlights, supplemented by radar directed anti-aircraft batteries, and backed up by twin engined Messerschmitt Bf 110 and Junkers Ju 88 nightfighters which flew circular patterns while waiting to intercept bombers attempting to cross the searchlight bands. The Kammhuber Line took an ever increasing toll of the British raiders who had to either penetrate the line or fly around it. However, flying around the Kammhuber Line became more difficult as the Line was extended to cover virtually the entire coast of Europe. Before long the Kammhuber Line was further strengthened with ground controlled radar-vectored nightfighters operating in circular zones just behind the line of searchlights and flak. After running the gauntlet of searchlights and flak the bombers then had to cross through the ground controlled radar directed fighter zones.

It was probably a ground controlled Bf 110 on the night of 7/8 July 1941 that swung up under Wellington 1C/L7818 of No 75 (New Zealand) Squadron. The bomber was one of forty aircraft from No 3 Group attacking Münster and had turned homeward when the 110's cannon shells smashed

(Above) A Wellington Mk 1C belonging to No 214 Squadron is seen at Stradishall during 1940. The scalloped camouflage pattern and markings are standard for this period of Bomber Command operations. R3209 went MIA on 8 December 1940 over Düsseldorf.

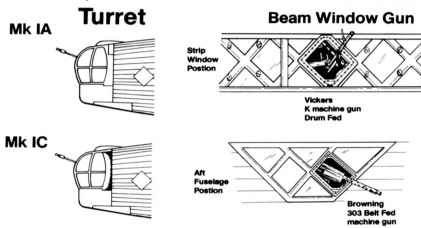

Turret — Beam Window Gun

Mk IA

Strip Window Postion

Vickers K machine gun Drum Fed

Mk IC

Aft Fuselage Postion

Browning 303 Belt Fed machine gun

(Below) A Mk 1C receiving its bomb load which includes a 1,000 pound bomb on the first trolley behind the towing tractor. The other trollies carry standard 250 pound bombs.

(Above Right) The slight cut back of the fuselage allowed the nose turret to fully traverse. The bomb-spitting devil and cheery smiles on the armorers faces belie the limited effect that Bomber Command's ordnance was having on German industry. The scene is believed to be at Feltwell, then the base for No 75 (New Zealand) Squadron.

into the fuselage and starboard wing starting a fire which defied all efforts to extinguish. The rear gunner's return fire sent the Bf 110 into a smoking dive. The apparently hopelessness of his bomber persuaded Squadron Leader Widdowson to order his crew to bale-out. However, the second pilot, Sergeant James Ward volunteered to climb out through the astrodome and onto the wing in an attempt to put out the fire with a canvas engine cover. The Wimpy was throttled back to minimum airspeed but even at this reduced speed the fierce slipstream constantly threatened to pull the twenty-two year old airman off the fabric surface. Sgt Ward used the fabric's pliancy by gouging holes in which to gain a grasp and maintain his precarious position in the sub-zero temperatures. The nearly frozen pilot managed to stuff the canvas engine cover into the area through which the fire was streaking but soon the physical exertion caused him to lose grip of it. His action, however, tipped the balance between disaster and salvation; as he was hauled back into the bomber the fire momentarily flared up, sputtered, then went out. Squadron Leader Widdowson set the Wellington IC down at Newmarket Heath without flaps or brakes. Such was the extent of the damage that the aircraft was subsequently declared a write-off. The Victoria Cross, Britain's highest military award was presented to Sgt Ward by King George VI, and was the sole example to be granted to a Wellington crew member. Sadly, the young flier was fated to die over Hamburg in X3205 two months later, becoming one of the 47,000 brave men of Bomber Command who gave their lives during operations over Europe.

(Left) Looking toward the cockpit inside the fuselage of a Mk 1C of No 99 Squadron provides an excellent view of the geodetic structure. The circular flare chute on the right and the Elsan chemical toilet on left are directly above the bomb-bay inspection panels. The circular shape at the bottom is a plate covering the opening where the deleted ventral turret would have been raised and lowered.

Mediterranean Theater

The Italian Declaration of War caught the RAF in the Western Desert woefully ill-equipped with only a few units flying medium-range Blenheims with low bomb-load capacity. Introduction of the Wellington into the Mediterranean Theater of Operations (MTO) provided a very potent aerial weapon beginning in September of 1940 when No 70 Squadron based at El Kabrit in the Suez Canal Zone began to re-equip with Wellington Mk 1As. This unit was soon joined by No 37 and 38 Squadrons who flew out from Britain in November. No 148 Squadron began Wellington operations from the strategically positioned island of Malta, operating from there from December of 1940 to the following March before joining the other three Wimpy units in Egypt. A fifth Canal Zone-based Squadron, No 108 Squadron, was equipped with Wellingtons upon its re-formation in August of 1941.

Detachments from these four Squadrons, at intervals during 1941, were sent to Malta, Crete and Iraq, while the main assault upon the Axis in the MTO was mounted from the Canal Zone and landing fields across the breadth of North Africa as the desert campaign see-sawed back and forth between the protagonists. From late 1941 No 40 Squadron supplemented the bombing effort from its Malta base. The effect on German and Italian forces of concerted bombing attacks on their seaports, supply bases and in particular upon their sea-borne traffic was out of all proportion to the number of Wellingtons deployed during this critical phase of the North African Campaign. Apart from No 38 Squadron which was transferred to torpedo-dropping duties in January of 1942 the Squadrons soldiered on with their Wellington Mk 1Cs well into 1942, when they were gradually replaced by Mk IIs and Mk IIIs, or in the case of No 108 Squadron by Liberators.

Lorenz Horizontal Receiving Aerial

(Below Left) This Mk 1C carries the original Bomber Command camouflage separation which is very low on the fuselage. Type A fuselage roundels, and what will become the standard Type B upper wing roundels, and carried on virtually all WW II British bombers can be seen painted on the aircraft. The Black under-surface color slightly overlaps onto the top surface of the wings in a wavy pattern.

(Above) This Wellington Mk IC (R1452) was fortunate to survive its crash landing at RAF Newton on 21 March 1941. The mound on which it precariously rests is Newton's bomb dump!

(Below Right) On 12 August 1941 'Rocky Victor' of No 75 (NZ) Squadron was shot up by a German nightfighter over the Zuider Zee and limped back to RAF Feltwell. While in the landing circuit at Feltwell the engines cut out. F/O Roberts, of the Royal Australian Air Force (RAAF), hurriedly baled out the rest of the crew and was fortunate enough to safely crash-land in a clearing in Thetford Forest. When the tail turret was rotated through the full ninety degrees it afforded the gunner a backward exit.

(Above Left) Holes in the fuselage and starboard wing of Mk 1C/L7818 are hand-holds gouged by Sgt James Ward when he crawled out on the wing in an attempt to put out the engine fire threatening to destroy the bomber. The Victoria Cross was awarded to the No 75 (New Zealand) Squadron pilot. Ward was KIA over Hamburg the following September.

(Below Left) Polish Wellington Squadrons were in the front-line of Bomber Command's night offensive and suffered accordingly. This crashed Wellington embedded in the beach sand at low tide belongs to No 301 (Pomeranian) Squadron, it was brought down on 26 June 1942, the third 'Thousand Bomber' raid to Bremen.

(Above Right) A Mk 1C (L7842) KX T of No 311 (Czech) Squadron in enemy hands. The lower Black areas of the fuselage and wings have been re-painted in Yellow, indicating that the bomber now belongs to the Luftwaffe Experimental and Test Unit at Rechlin. The aircraft force-landed in 1940 but its ultimate fate is unknown.

(Below Right) A wealth of detail is visible as this Mk 1C is stripped down by WAAFs at what is believed to be a Coastal Command airfield. The Pegasus aircooled engine can be seen to good advantage and below it the exhaust pipe with the heating muff attached can be seen. The code letters appear to be HR but cannot be traced to a specific unit, although some records suggest the possible allocation to No 304 (Polish) Squadron.

(Above Left) This pair of Wimpys at Mildenhall display variations in fin flashes and fuselage roundels. The extension of the Black camouflage onto upper part of the fuselage between wing and tailplane was seen on a large number of Wellingtons during the 1940/41 period. The towing tractor is a Fordson design and much used by the RAF.

(Below Left) Incendiary containers and 250 pound bombs are rather casually strewn under this Wimpy. The outer bomb cells have two doors, while the center cell has only one door hinged on the port beam. The navigation/identification light is mounted just ahead of the inwardly opening crew hatch. The circular shape on the port side of the belly is the blind-flying panel Venturi. The stick shapes protruding above starboard bomb-door are winching rods to which crank-handles were attached when raising bombs into the bomb-bay.

(Above Right) Servicing of this No 214 Squadron Wellington at Stradishall appears to be more for the photographer's benefit than for the aircraft's benefit. The gunner's entrance/escape doors of the nose turret are open, and the spinner has been removed exposing the air ducts used to cool the Pegasus engine.

(Below) FLN (T2501) of 99 Squadron after being forced down on the continent. No 99 Squadron transferred to India during early 1942, using their Wellington 1Cs against the Japanese in Burma

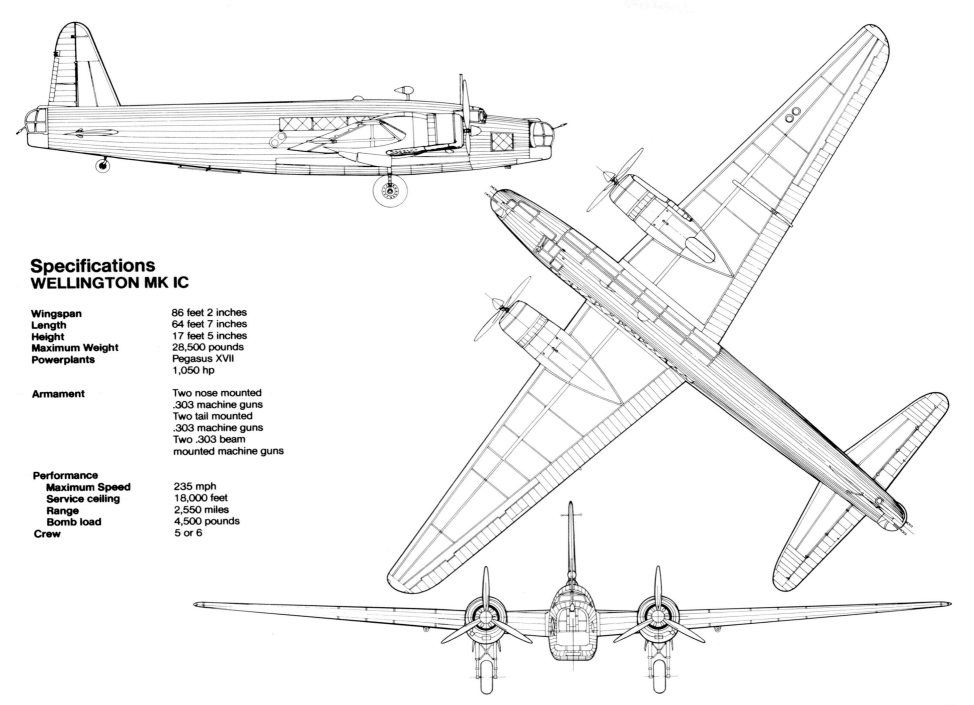

Specifications
WELLINGTON MK IC

Wingspan	86 feet 2 inches
Length	64 feet 7 inches
Height	17 feet 5 inches
Maximum Weight	28,500 pounds
Powerplants	Pegasus XVII
	1,050 hp
Armament	Two nose mounted
	.303 machine guns
	Two tail mounted
	.303 machine guns
	Two .303 beam
	mounted machine guns
Performance	
Maximum Speed	235 mph
Service ceiling	18,000 feet
Range	2,550 miles
Bomb load	4,500 pounds
Crew	5 or 6

(Above) Incendiary cases and 250 pound bombs on trolleys ready for loading into this Mk 1C of No 301 (Polish) Squadron at Swinderby. The serial number is carried in a camouflage box just ahead of the horizontal stabilizer.

(Right) A Mk 1C Wimpy of No 304 (Polish) Squadron with a combined bomb and depth charge load in the foreground. The squadron transferred from Bomber Command to Coastal Command in May of 1942. The unit's anti-submarine record included forty-three 'sightings', of which thirty-four ended in attacks, out of a total of 2,451 sorties that were flown.

(Below) Mk 1C/HD975 ('L Love') was ferried out to join No 99 Squadron in India during late 1942. Pilot Officer T H Claridge departed Moreton-in-the-Marsh on 30 September, reaching Digri in Bengal on 29 October, with a flying time of 95 hours 5 minutes. The aircraft is seen at a stop-over base in West Africa. The nose turret has been removed to save weight.

(Above) Three Mk ICs of No 311 Squadron, the sole Czech representative in Bomber Command, during March of 1941. Blacking over of the White roundel area was done to reduce the ability of German searchlights to pick out the bombers. The squadron was flying out of East Wretham, but transferred to Coastal Command in April 1942. The nearest two aircraft were posted MIA during mid-1942, while KX K crashed during landing on 18 March 1941.

(Below Left) Flight Officer Gregory and Sgt Billington (inside of fuselage) of No 149 Squadron inspect the damage to their Mk 1C/X9746. During a mission to Duisburg on 18 August 1941 cannon shells blasted the rear area and the resulting fire was fought for fifteen minutes by Billington who, despite being drenched by oil from his turret, fought the blaze with his hands and parachute! Immediate DFC and DFM awards were granted to Gregory and Billington respectively.

(Below Right) Rear view of 'A' Able demonstrates the ruggedness of the geodetic structure of the Wellington. The twin navigation lights on the upper part of the rudder are prominent.

(Above) Looking remarkably fresh for an operationally retired aircraft this Mk 1C is seen at El Kabrit in the Suez Canal Zone on 29 March 1943. The beam gun window is just forward of the fuselage roundel which has been re-painted to the type C1 standard as is the fin flash.

(Below Left) 'L London' of No 70 Squadron was attacked by a Ju 88 while trying to land on 25 April 1942. Caught at a most vulnerable landing stage when downwind with gear and flaps down, the starboard elevator was shot off and both tires were punctured, but P/O Mansell got the plane down and the crew survived the assault. The aircraft is seen at El Kabrit the following day.

(Below Right) 'K' of No 37 Squadron on Malta awaits being loaded with 250 pound bombs. This unit operated Wimpys in the Middle East from late 1940 to 1944, and its Malta based detachment played a vital part in harassing Axis sea-borne traffic, as well as bombing targets in Sicily and Italy.

WELLINGTON DWI

Directional Wireless Installation (DWI)

Shortly after the British declaration of War the Germans began laying magnetic sea mines from low flying aircraft and U-Boats in British coastal waters, especially in the south east area. These mines were anchored to the sea bottom with weights and were detonated by the metal hulls of ships. No immediate solution was found and Allied shipping losses quickly mounted. One of the mines was successfully recovered and defused, revealing their inner workings, allowing British scientists to devise two methods of neutralization. A passive method of neutralizing the mines lay in equipping ships with degaussing gear to nullify the magnetic attraction of the ship's steel hull; ironically Professor Gauss was a German. An aggressive method of dealing with the mines was to destroy them by triggering their detonator by creating a magnetic field.

Vickers was approached to modify a number of Wellingtons to carry equipment consisting of generators with which to create an electro magnetic field generated from an aluminum coil encased inside a cumbersome circular 51 foot diameter balsa wood structure outside the aircraft. The anticipated aerodynamic problems of this arrangement proved less than initially feared. The balsa casing was constructed in sections and the assembly minus the aluminum coil was slung under a Wellington Mk IA (P2516) for flight testing. After the flight characteristics tests proved satisfactory the aluminum strip coil was inserted. The nose and tail turrets were removed and faired into smooth conical positions, later some aircraft carried glazed tail positions. To save weight the interiors were generally stripped of all unnecessary equipment.

The aluminum strip coils were initially powered with a Ford V8 engine driving 35 kw Maudsley generators. Three more Wellington Mk 1As were modified straight off the Vickers Weybridge production line, however, the pressure of both production and experimental work at the main Vickers plant forced conversion work on some eleven additional Mk Is to be carried out at Croydon with Rollasons performing airframe adaptation and English Electric producing the coils.

The lighter, but more powerful Gypsy Six motor driving a 95 kw generator were installed under the designation of Wellington DWI Mk II. The Gypsy's 95 KW output generated a much greater magnetic field while saving over 1,000 pounds of weight.

Tests carried out on the magnetic section of a de-fused German mine located in the middle of the experimental airfield at Boscombe Down provided encouraging results, however, there were several factors which had to be taken into account before practical results could be realized. Tidal depth affected the degree of magnetic field which could be directed at the mine.

Another critical factor in searching out and destroying a mine was the height at which the aircraft could safely descend without the risk of being damaged by the mine's detonation. Initial operational flights were conducted at around 60 feet, however, it was felt that 35 feet was the minimum altitude. The speed of the aircraft had to be slow enough that the magnetic field did not peak for too short a period of time to detonate the mine, but fast enough that detonation of a mine did not damage the aircraft. Also, the angle of incidence of the magnetic ring had to be co-ordinated with the trim of the aircraft in order to bring to bear the most effective electro magnetic field on a mine. The first aerial detonation of a mine was achieved on 8 January 1940, however, prior to this a mine had been detonated by the specialist vessel Borde, but the ship was badly damaged in the process and the task of mine detonation was left to the Wimpys of No 1 GRU. The second recorded aerial success was five days later on 13 January, but on this occasion the aircraft descended below 35 feet, the hatches were blown off and the accelerometer recorded ten Gs. The aircraft was grounded and checked by Vickers engineers for structural damage. None was found, confirming the strength of the geodetic structure of the Wimpy's design.

Due to the presence of the DWI gear normal compasses were thought to be completely inoperable and recourse was to the use of the standard air-driven Gyro Direction Indicator (GDI). The GDI had to be set using a stretch of straight railway track laid out in the vicinity of the Manston base from which operations were conducted. Subsequently, P4 compasses were located in the aircraft tail well away from structural influences, doing away with dependence on the fallible GDI. After operations began a directional switch was installed which allowed a reversal of the direction of the coil's electrical current

(Above) The unmistakably distinctive plan view of a DWI Wellington passing overhead.

DWI Installation

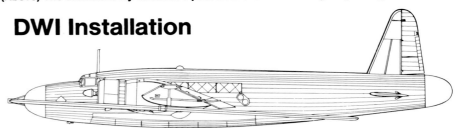

from the normal North-seeking thrust to South-seeking in order to detonate mines whose magnetism was so set.

The two trial DWI Wimpys (P2518 and P2521) carried out initial sweeps and were soon joined by the first Gypsy Six equipped Wellington DWI Mk II (L4356) and plans were put into effect for a series of combined aircraft sweeps to increase the magnetic field. The rate of mine destruction was steady rather than spectacular and the inclusion of Wellington DWI Mk IIs within the force was of definite advantage. In April a second GRU unit was formed and based at Bircham Newton in Norfolk. The operation of the generators produced heat discomfort for the actual operator, but the provision of air ducts did considerably reduce the temperature. Ducts were also used in cooling the smaller 48 foot diameter ring of the DWI Mk II.

Since DWI aircraft were defenseless a fighter was assigned to protect, them with the Blenheims of No 600 Squadron drawing the duty, however, in the event no recorded attack by the Luftwaffe was made. The enemy was advancing through the Low Countries and France in its successful May offensive.

One of the Wellington DWI Mk Is (L4374) was detached on 20 May to the Middle East where its use after the Italian entry into the War was to lead to the conversion of several Mk IAs and a single Mk IC to DWI aircraft for sweeping duties around the Suez Canal. Parts were sent out from Britain for the conversions. Ironically, as the British advanced across the desert during 1942/43 DWI Wellingtons were used to sweep North African ports of not only German mines, but also of British mines!

(Above Left) Believed to be in Suez Canal Zone this DWI Wellington has its ring set out on the hanger floor ready for installation onto the aircraft. The conical brace on the nose is the ring's forward attachment pylon.

(Above Right) This Wellington Mk IC was modified to DWI standards and operated by No 1 GRU at Ismailia dug into the sand during a forced landing at El Ballah. The precise function of the camel tethered to the ring is unknown. The tilted-up angle of the ring in relation to the fuselage can seen.

Wellington DWI Installation

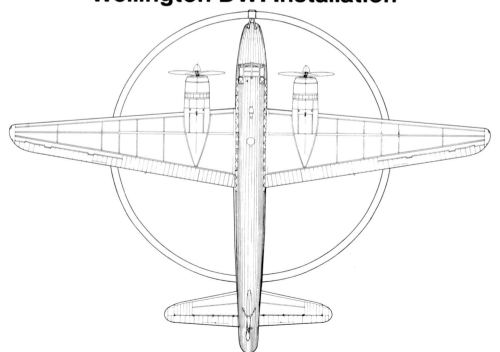

(Below Right) After being dug out of the sand and minor repairs made, the DWI Wellington was flown out.

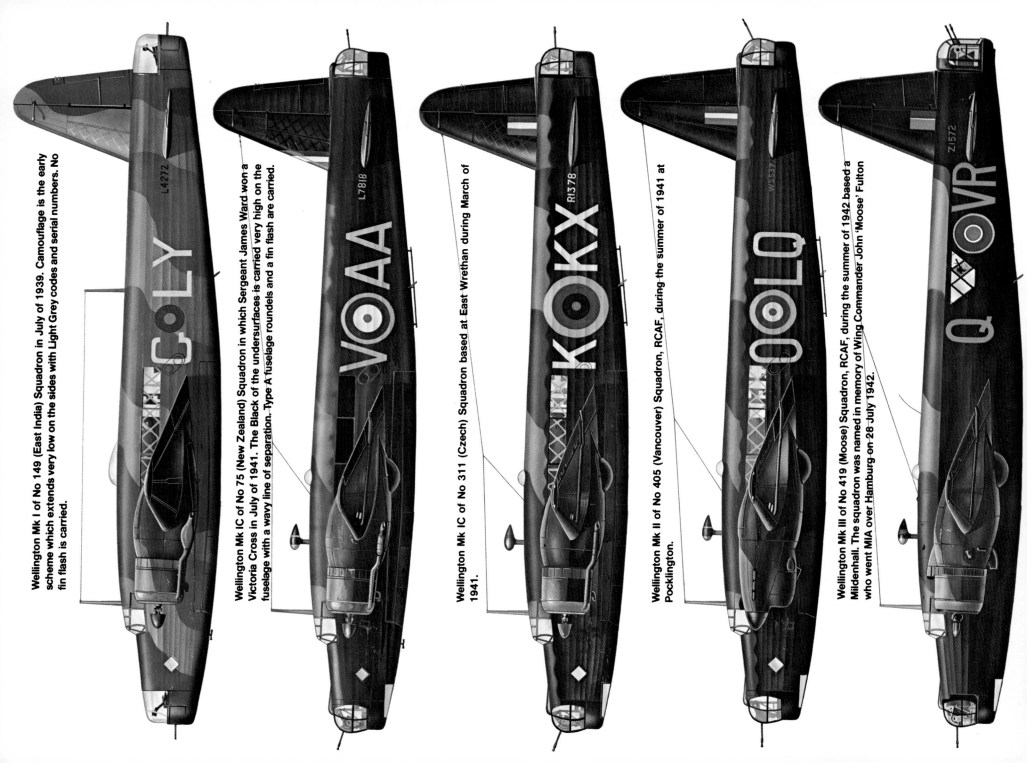

Wellington Mk I of No 149 (East India) Squadron in July of 1939. Camouflage is the early scheme which extends very low on the sides with Light Grey codes and serial numbers. No fin flash is carried.

Wellington Mk IC of No 75 (New Zealand) Squadron in July of 1941. The Black of the undersurfaces is carried very high on the fuselage with a wavy line of separation. Type A fuselage roundels and a fin flash are carried. Sergeant James Ward won a Victoria Cross in which Sergeant James Ward won a Victoria Cross in July of 1941.

Wellington Mk IC of No 311 (Czech) Squadron based at East Wrethan during March of 1941.

Wellington Mk II of No 405 (Vancouver) Squadron, RCAF, during the summer of 1941 at Pocklington.

Wellington Mk III of No 419 (Moose) Squadron, RCAF, during the summer of 1942 based a Mildenhall. The squadron was named in memory of Wing Commander John 'Moose' Fulton who went MIA over Hamburg on 28 July 1942.

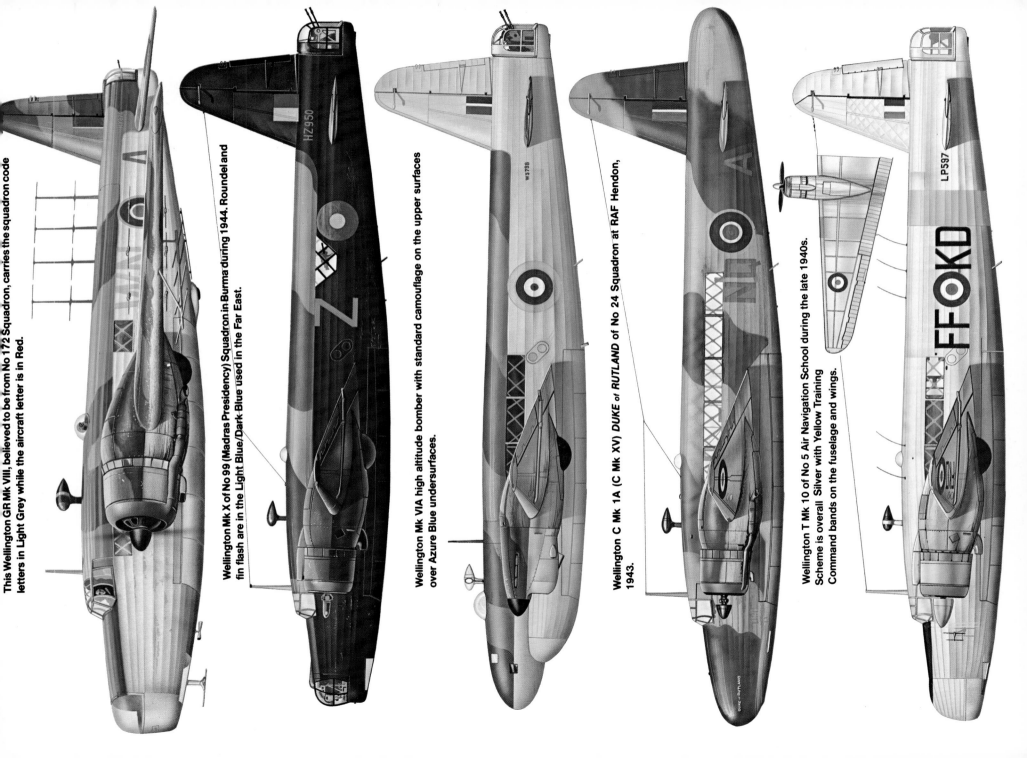

This Wellington GR Mk VIII, believed to be from No 172 Squadron, carries the squadron code letters in Light Grey while the aircraft letter is in Red.

Wellington Mk X of No 99 (Madras Presidency) Squadron in Burma during 1944. Roundel and fin flash are in the Light Blue/Dark-Blue used in the Far East.

Wellington Mk VIA high altitude bomber with standard camouflage on the upper surfaces over Azure Blue undersurfaces.

Wellington C Mk 1A (C Mk XV) *DUKE of RUTLAND* of No 24 Squadron at RAF Hendon, 1943.

Wellington T Mk 10 of No 5 Air Navigation School during the late 1940s. Scheme is overall Silver with Yellow Training Command bands on the fuselage and wings.

Wellington GR Mk VIII

From the beginning, the war at sea was as fierce and unremitting as the war in the air, and nowhere was it as concentrated and vital during the six years of hostilities than it was in the North Atlantic. During the first years of the war a lack of escort vessels, radar, and other search equipment with which to seek out and destroy German U-boats gave the Kreigsmarine a deadly edge. Multi-engined aircraft were sorely needed to help the Allied Navies redress this imbalance by patrolling and attacking U-Boats.

Radar equipped multi-engine aircraft were also sorely needed to patrol the sealanes searching out and attacking enemy surface shipping, especially in the Mediterranean Theater where German and Italian forces in North Africa were supplied almost exclusively by sea. To provide a patrol aircraft to solve both the surface shipping and submarine threats the Mk IC was modified to carry ASV II search radar under the designation Wellington GR Mk VIII and was developed in both day and night variants. The day variant being an anti-shipping torpedo bomber and the night variant being an anti-submarine bomber.

Wellington GR Mk VIII Torpedo Bomber

ASV Mk II *Stickleback* radar was fitted to 271 Wimpys which were all adaptations of standard Wellington Mk 1C airframes, and other than the fitting of numerous aerials to the GR Mk VIII, was externally essentially similar to the Mk IC.

Use of the Wellington Mk VIII torpedo bomber was largely concentrated in the Mediterranean Theater where the enemy's dependence on shipping men and material to the Afrika Korps was of paramount importance. The island of Malta lay astride most sea routes between Europe and North Africa and GR Mk VIIIs based there sank or crippled numerous vessels during the crucial months surrounding the Battle of El Alamein in October of 1942. The outcome of this crucial North African battle was undoubtedly tipped to the British 8th Army by the enemy's men and material lying at the bottom of the sea

Wellington GR Mk VIII Anti-Submarine

By 1940/41 airborne radar equipment was available in quantity but had a limiting factor when used over water. A target could be picked up at range, but due to echoes off of the water the target was lost during the run-up just before visual contact could be made. This vital loss of the target during the aircraft's last mile, was to be brilliantly and simply solved with the use of a searchlight carried within the aircraft itself. The searchlight concept was the brain-child of Squadron Leader Humphrey De Verde Leigh, a First World War pilot who was now an Administrative Officer.

The test platform for this innovative scheme was a redundant DWI Wellington equipped with a generator supplying the power for the searchlight. Leigh at first considered the use of a 90 CM army searchlight but quickly turned his attention to the more compact and lighter 60 CM naval searchlight which fit neatly into the retractable housing of the deleted ventral turret which could be raised and lowered through the belly aperture. Using the hydraulic system designed by Frazer Nash for its gun turrets whose manipulation was extremely precise and capable of both vertical and horizontal movement.

Air ducted through a fairing on the aircraft's underside provided ventilation to dissipate the tremendous heat generated by the searchlight, and a rotating cowl focused rearward by the slipstream funneled air across the light pulling out the fumes. The bulky generator was subsequently replaced by seven 12 volt batteries, saving both weight and space in the crowded fuselage.

A scheme of Group Captain Helmore, whose nose-mounted light had been pioneered on Boston nightfighters, was offered as an alternative to the Leigh Light. However the Helmore Light being mounted in the nose was in a direct line of crew vision creating a glare problem. In contrast the Leigh Light being mounted in a retractable turret on the belly threw its beam below the crew's line of vision, and just as importantly allowed the light operator an unobstructed view from his nose position. Results of comparative tests using Wellingtons ES986 (Leigh Light) and T2977 (Helmore Light) seemed to be in

(Above) A GR Mk VIII Wellington flying at about the 50 foot height at which the Leigh Light (now retracted) was most effective. The aircraft carries the early Coastal Command scheme of Grey/Green top colors over White sides and under-surfaces. The code letters are an unusual mix of Light Grey and Red. The four ASV Mk II aerials on the spine of the fuselage and clear nose canopy can be clearly seen. The Type C1 markings indicate the the aircraft is seen during the latter part of 1942. The aircraft is believed to be from No 172 Squadron but no definite allocation of the WN code letters can be confirmed.

favor of the Leigh Light. However, the C in C of Coastal Command came to the opposite conclusion, but soon changed his mind.

Squadron Leader Leigh was privileged to carry out the first successful trials of his apparatus when Submarine H-31 of the Royal Navy was illuminated on 4 May 1941 in the Irish Sea. During evaluation naval officers from the submarine testified that the bomber was not spotted until the light was turned on, at which point there was minimal time for the submarine to evade attack.

In addition to the 271 radar equipped Wellington GR Mk VIII day torpedo bombers the surprisingly small number of only fifty-eight aircraft were fitted with the Leigh Light as anti-submarine aircraft. While those ASV Mk II equipped GR Mk VIIIs operated primarily as torpedo bombers retained both the front and rear turrets, Leigh Light equipped aircraft had the nose turret removed and the light operator was provided with a clear canopy similar to the earlier Wellington Mk I, through which he was able to both sight and track his target.

No 172 Squadron was chosen to pioneer the Leigh Light in service. Based at Chivenor in southwest England, the GR Mk VIIIs crew complement was non-standard, being made up of two fully qualified pilots, a navigator and three wireless operators/aerial gunners. During run-up to the target the navigator was expected to turn on the searchlight, man the nose guns and release the depth charges! In order to extend the aircraft's operational endurance the normal 750 gallon fuel capacity was supplemented by fuel tanks fitted into the outer bomb cells while six depth charges were carried in the center cell.

U-Boats had usually run on the surface at night while crossing the Bay of Biscay both because their surface speed was greater than when submerged and to charge their batteries. The U-Boat's immunity from attack at night dramatically disappeared with the introduction of the radar and searchlight combination. The first successful interception of an enemy submarine occurred on 4 June

1942 when an Italian submarine was badly damaged, though not sunk. No 179 Squadron was soon in action alongside No 172 Squadron and the use of radio altimeters was now providing very accurate indication of the 50 foot height at which the Light beam should be turned on in order to pick out a U-Boat; No 172 Squadron had previously missed several conclusive engagements due to the absence of precise altitude information. On 5 July Pilot/Officer Howell, an American who had joined the RAF prior to Pearl Harbor, scored the first confirmed kill when he sank U-502 in the act of battery-discharge while crossing the Bay of Biscay. Although the number of confirmed successes was destined to be relatively small, the effect on German Naval morale was disproportionately high until the Germans developed a mobile radar unit which provided enough warning for a U-Boat to crash-dive in time to avoid an attack.

Wellington GR Mk VIII Bombers
A third batch of sixty-five aircraft were delivered into service as bombers and were essentially similar to the torpedo bomber variant.

Nose Development

Mk IC

ASV II Fuselage Aerials (Stickle back)

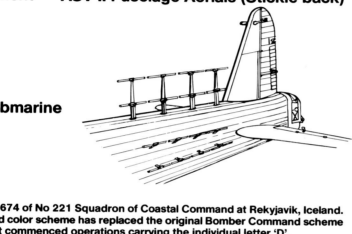

Mk VIII Anti-submarine

(Below Left) DF O/W5674 of No 221 Squadron of Coastal Command at Rekyjavik, Iceland. The Coastal Command color scheme has replaced the original Bomber Command scheme with which the aircraft commenced operations carrying the individual letter 'D'.

(Above Right) This GR Mk VIII HX602, 'P Peter' of No 38 Squadron, is seen at El Kabrit Egypt during 1943. Many Wimpys converted to patrol duties in the MTO had their nose turrets faired over, and may have been an indication of the reduced chances of aerial interception while conducting low-level sea searches in the Mediterranean.

Wing Aerials

Starboard Wing

Port Wing

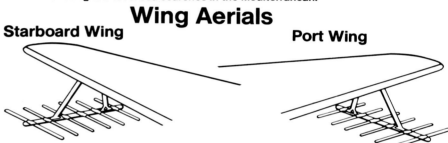

(Below Right) BB466 of No 458 (RAAF) Squadron was another Mk 1C converted to GR Mk VIII specifications. Seen at Shandur in North Africa during 1943 it carries the standard Bomber Command color scheme and Type C1 roundels are carried.

WELLINGTON MK II

Anticipating the possibility of a shortage of Pegasus powerplants as well as to allow for the use of more powerful engines as they became available two Mk I airframes (L4250 and L4251) were equipped with Merlin and Hercules powerplants. The 1145 hp Merlin X was installed in L4250 and the 1425 hp Hercules III was installed in L4251. The oil-cooled inline Merlin engines were of considerably greater weight and resurrected the Wellington's Center of Gravity and nose heaviness problems, which were again solved by increasing the elevator mass-balance and the tailplane span.

Carrying an FN5 nose and FN10 tail turret L4250 flew for the first time with Merlin engines Rotol propellers with wooden Jablo blades on 3 March 1939. All-up weight of the Wellington Mk II, of which 401 would be built at Weybridge, was 33,000 pounds, an increase of 4,500 pounds over the Mk 1C. This increase in power and gross weight inevitably affected the aircraft's performance at operational altitude, maximum speed was increased to 254 mph, range was reduced by between 330 and 350 miles, and bombload was reduced by 500 pounds. The increase in ceiling from the 18,000 feet of the Mk IC to 23,500 of the Mk II was vital to the vulnerable bombers trying to evade the flak and fighters of the Kammhuber Line.

Other than the engines there were no obvious external differences when compared with previous Wimpy Marks. The diamond shaped window on the starboard side of the nose was blanked out on many Mk IIs, however not all. The Wellington Mk II began coming into front-line service during the Winter of 1940/41 by which time the RAF was also receiving the first of what was to become its standard heavy explosive bomb, the 4,000 pound 'Cookie' or 'Blockbuster'. The girth of this new bomb was such that it was incapable of being accommodated within the normal Wellington bomb-bay, however the modification of Mk II/W5389 with Type 423 gear proved successful. From the available evidence it appears that the center sections of the bomb-bay were removed, but since the bomb-doors would still not close when the bomb was in place portions of the doors were also removed. In quick succession W5442, W5452, Z8373 and Z8490 were similarly modified and dispatched to No 214 Squadron, where five Mk ICs already on strength also had their bomb-bays modified. The first use of the 4,000 pound bomb, which would become a major tool in the night bombing offensive, was against city of Emden on the night of 1 April 1941. The results were devastating.

Wellingtons, had been in use in the Western Desert since September of 1940, when the Mk IAs and ICs initially sent out, were joined and in some cases supplanted by the Merlin powered Wellington Mk II. Squadrons known to have used the Mark II during their time in the MTO included No 37, 40, 104 and 108 Squadrons. Rommel's supply dumps and seaports were kept under constant pressure by Wimpy units. One of the most frequented targets was Benghazi, and such was the frequency of raids that it was dubbed the *Mail Run*. Indeed, No 70 Squadron personnel created a song which described their experiences on the *Run* which was sung to the tune of *Clementine*. The Mk II also played a heavy role in harassing Axis sea traffic. The Wellington was a central player in the multitude of tasks carried out by the RAF in the MTO between 1940 and 1942.

After trials as the Mk II test-bed were completed towards the end of 1940, L4250 was selected as the test-bed for installing the Vickers 40 MM gun which was a heavy caliber weapon intended for installation in the B1/39 specification bomber. 20 MM cannon were initially planned for this design with four being mounted in each turret but their replacement by the 40 MM unit was proposed. Installation in L4250 was limited to a dorsal turret with a single 40 MM gun, but created a dangerous aerodynamic problem when the turret's bulky shape caused severe vibration and turbulence due to the airflow pattern thrown against the standard fin. To cure this difficulty the upper sections of two fins were mounted on the outer tail plane surfaces, braced by struts attached to the fuselage. This adaptation alleviated, if it did not cure the problem totally. A number of test flights were conducted, but the Vickers cannon turret was not put into production. Wellington Z8416 was used to test the Vickers 'S' gun of a similar caliber in a nose-mounted location.

The Wellington Mk II was also used for several years to test jet engines. Tail mounted Whittle jet engines were carried by W5389/G and Z8570/G with the former also bearing Merlin 62 engines and the later Mk VI wings were installed allowing the aircraft to attain a height of 36,000 feet.

(Above) The Wellington Mk II prototype (L4250), which apart from the installation of the Merlin X engines is a Wellington Mk I, its un-faired DF loop and twin aerial masts being still in place. Later, after being used as a test aircraft for the Vickers 40 MM gun, in December of 1942 the ship passed to a School of Technical Training for use as a ground instruction machine only.

(Below) This Mk II of No 214 Squadron at Stradishall during 1941 is believed to have been converted to carry the 4,000 pound 'Cookie' blast bomb. A tiger's head and the inscription *SRI GUROH* was carried just below the cockpit, denoting the Squadron's ties with the Federated Malay States.

(Above Left) Armorers manhandle a trolley loaded with 250 pound bombs to gaping bomb-bay doors in the belly of a No 405 (RCAF) Squadron Wimpy Mk II. The distinctively sharp outlines of the Jablo wooden propellers fitted to the in-line Merlin powerplants are silhouetted against a bright afternoon sky.

Engine Development

Mk IC   DeHavilland Hamilton

Pegasus XVII Engine

DeHavilland Hamilton Propellors

Mk II   Rotol Propellors

Merlin X Engine

Rotol Propellors

(Right) This badly bent Mk II appears to have left the crew with a largely intact fuselage in which to survive the crash-landing near Hatfield, Herts. The aircraft is under rather close scrutiny by a mixture of RAF and civilian personnel.

(Above Right) No 405 Squadron was one of the few RCAF units to operate the Merlin powered Wellington Mk II. The forward fuselage windows have been blanked out around their edges while the nose side window has been totally blanked out. The horse pulling a plough in the background is a rather peaceful contrast with this aerial instrument of war. Many airfields were located amongst farms, and the space between the runways was often put under cultivation, sometimes by RAF Personnel.

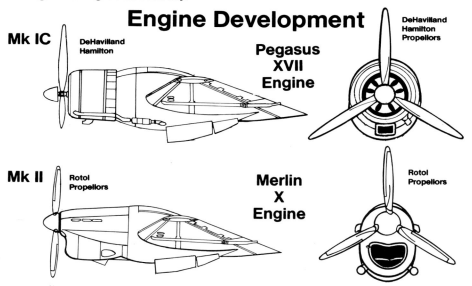

(Above Left) The stocky low-slung profiles of three Wellington Mk IIs of No 405 Squadron are armed and waiting for the darkness which has become their natural environment.

(Above Right) LQ E of No 405 Squadron is eased onto its final approach as a fellow Wimpy taxies round the perimeter track at either Pocklington or Topcliffe, Yorks during the summer of 1941. The squadron relinquished their Mk IIs for Halifaxes in the following April.

(Below) Z8597 of No 104 Squadron taxiing out at El Kabrit on 3 December 1942. The squadron codes on MTO bombers were usually discarded, and most certainly while operating out of North Africa. This aircraft was MIA over the island of Pantellaria on 11 June 1943. A B-24D Liberator carrying the early star with a Blue surround can be seen in the far left background.

(Above) The Mk II prototype was later used to test the Vickers 40 mm gun. The bulky turret caused critical airflow problems around the standard Wellington vertical fin.

(Below Left) To solve the problem a revised tail unit using the top halves of two different fins was installed. This modification was fitted with three bracing rods on each fin, and the rear turret was faired over. The lower fuselage is painted Yellow which found on most RAF prototype aircraft.

(Below Right) The 40 mm had a rather clumsy slot mounting in the turret as well as the aerodynamically clumsy fin-bracing.

WELLINGTON MK III

Parallel with the oil-cooled inline Merlin engined Mk II, was the Wellington Mk III powered by a pair of 1,425 hp aircooled Hercules III radial powerplants. For some time Vickers had been working on an increase in power for the Wellington, the result was the Wellington Mk III Hercules whose power output exceeded the Pegasus engine by 375 hp. While the installation of both the Hercules III and the parallel developed Hercules XI engine were destined not to improve the Wellington's range or bombload capacity the new radials did provide an additional 3,500 feet in maximum altitude over that of the Mk 1. Production was almost evenly split between Chester (737) and Blackpool (780), only two were produced at Weybridge.

The Wellington Mk III prototype, Mk I/L4251 powered by Hercules HE1SM engines with two-stage superchargers and DeHavilland propellers, flew for the first time on 19 May 1939. Unsatisfactory performance of the DeHavilland propellers led to Mk 1C/P9328 being equipped with Hercules III engines driving Rotol propellers, with this machine coming to be regarded as the production prototype.

Other features which became standard were de-icing gear, balloon cutters and windshield wipers. A low drag FN21A ventral turret was mooted but not fitted. Instead the mock-up of a four gun FN20A turret was installed in the tail while the FN5 nose turret and beam guns remained unchanged. The new and more powerful four gun FN20 tail turret was first carried around March 1940 by L4251.

Entering service with No 9 Squadron on 22 June 1941 the Wellington Mk III was destined to be the backbone of Bomber Command and shouldered most of the night offensive load until such time as the four engined Stirlings, Halifaxes and Lancasters appeared in sufficient numbers to take over.

Additional features of the Mk III was its ability to tow gliders of all types up to the huge Airspeed Horsa, and the Mk III's capacity to transport up to ten fully equipped soldiers. A number of Mk IIIs were utilized in the early stages of training the British Army's Parachute Brigades. The ventral turret fairing was removed, providing a suitable exit for the trainee parachutists.

The arrival in February 1942 of Air Marshal Arthur 'Butch' Harris as Commander-in-Chief of Bomber Command would prove a godsend for the proponents of the strategic bombing theory. The night offensive had been going badly astray. The demands of the Royal Navy upon Bomber Command to divert aircraft for the anti-submarine campaign had especially dissipated Bomber Command's strategic assets. Not only was Bomber Command being distracted from its primary task, but in the face of increased German defenses losses, were mounting. The Luftwaffe was getting good at picking off individual bombers crossing the Kammhuber Line.

Air Marshal Harris set about convincing both skeptics and supporters among both the military and politicians, that there were very good reasons to leave his command severely alone. To do this Harris had to prove beyond any doubt that Bomber Command was capable of inflicting tremendous damage on the enemy. To this end he set in motion a plan that at first seemed so far fetched that it was almost ludicrous — to put one thousand bombers over a single target in a single night — and hopefully, utterly destroy it.

It would be weeks before the plan could be put into operation, time that was used to gather forces and work out tactics. The small number of Gee equipped Wellingtons were pressed into a basic Pathfinder force that would arrive over the target ahead of the main force, marking it with colored flares or incendiaries for the following bombers to aim at. One of the founding members of the Pathfinder Force in August 1942 was No 156 Squadron which was flying Wellingtons.

To concentrate the largest number of bombers over a target in the shortest length of time the **bomber stream** concept was born. These tactics were first used against Essen on the night of 8/9 March when 211 aircraft mostly Wellingtons attacked this main Ruhr target with limited success. On the night of 28/29 March 234 aircraft attacked Lübeck mostly with incendiaries. A total of 191 aircraft claimed to have attacked the target: damage was heavy, 1000 dwellings were destroyed and 4000 were damaged, 520 civilians were killed and 785 were injured. Eight bombers were lost. For four consecutive nights, 24/27 April Rostock was attacked. At the end of the fourth night sixty percent of the city was smoldering ruins. For the first time the Germans began using the term *Terror Raid*.

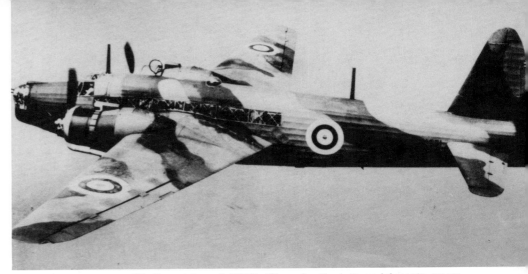

(Above) The Wellington Mk III prototype (L4251) still carries the twin aerial masts, an unfaired DF loop, and the continuous fuselage window strip, all of which reveals the aircraft's Mk I origin. The DeHavilland 'bracket' type of propellers were replaced by Rotol props on production machines. The aircraft is painted in the Type B camouflage scheme and a variation of the Type AI roundel is carried on the wings.

With hard results backing him Air Marshal Harris laid his plan before Sir Charles Portal, anticipating Bomber Command supplying 700 aircraft and the other commands supplying the rest. In the event the other Commands supplied almost nothing. Amazingly, however, Bomber Command, by completely stripping its Operational Training Units (OTUs), was able to put the unbelievable force of 1042 aircraft into the air. Under the code name OPERATION MILLENNIUM the Rhine river city of Cologne was chosen for the biggest and most dangerous Bomber Command undertaking of the war. Harris was risking not only his entire operational force but his entire training command as well. Wellingtons made up 599 aircraft of the raiding force.

At 00.47 the first bombs began falling on Cologne, and continued until 02.25 when the last bombs fell. 898 crews claimed to have attacked the target, delivering some 1445 tons of bombs. Over 600 acres of Cologne was destroyed, 486 people were killed, 5,027 were injured, and almost 60,000 were homeless. Fires burned for days. Bomber Command lost forty aircraft. No longer would Bomber Command be compelled to dissipate its force.

Early in the War the Canadian Government decreed that it would provide a full Group of bomber Squadrons and by 1943 no less than fourteen Squadrons constituted No 6 (Canadian) Group which was based in the North of England. By March of 1943 no fewer than six Squadrons within No 6 Group were flying Wellingtons, with No 429 (Canadian) Squadron was operating Wellington Mk IIIs in No 4 Group until April of 1943 when it converted to the Wellington Mk X. The Wellington Mk III's service as a front-line bomber extended well into 1943 and the beginning of massed bomber streams wreaking destruction on German cities, until it was supplanted by its four engined successors, the Stirling, Halifax, and Lancaster. On 8 October 1943 the Wellington Mk III flew its last mission.

While the Dambusters raid on 16/17 May 1943 was carried out by Lancasters, the initial tests of delivering the cylindrical mine used to destroy the dams were conducted in December of 1942 by Wellington Mk III/BJ895 which was specially modified to carry two of the scaled-down weapons. BK537 was used by Rotol in tests of the Company's airscrews while X3224 was utilized by the Royal Aircraft Establishment for engine cooling experiments. Retirement from Bomber Command ranks did not mean the Wellington Mk III had no other function, large numbers were to be used at the many training units dotting Britain.

(Above Left) The Mk III was the first Hercules-powered Wellington. The 'KO' unit codes indicate that X3662 served with No 115 Squadron. Type C1 roundels and late-pattern fin flash dates the aircraft at mid to late 1942. The tally of thirty-six bomb mission symbols on the nose is all the more impressive since the average bomber survival rate was eleven missions. The Squadron converted to Lancaster Mk IIs in March of 1943.

(Above Right) KW E (X3763) is a Mk III of No 425 (Alouette) Squadron RCAF. The short carburetor air-intakes, propeller hubs without spinners, and triangular beam gun windows were features on many Mk IIIs. The paint is peeling badly on the vertical fin. This bomber was MIA over Stuttgart on the night of 14/15 April 1943 by which time its individual aircraft code letter was changed to 'L'.

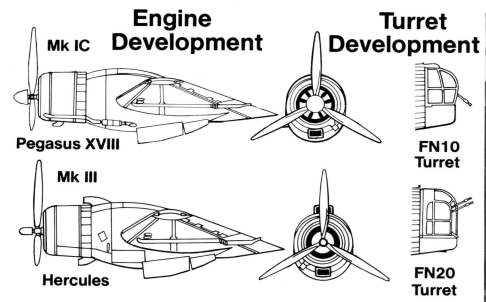

Engine Development

Mk IC

Pegasus XVIII

Mk III

Hercules

Turret Development

FN10 Turret

FN20 Turret

(Right) Used in the Dambuster program this Wellington Mk III (BJ895) carries two of the 'Dambuster' dummy mines in a specially adapted bomb-bay. The bomb-support frames contain a drive facility with which to spin the bombs prior to release. Tests were made in December of 1942 off Chesil Beach in Dorset. 'Golf ball' indentations can be seen on the rear bomb-casing.

A standard RAF fuel bowser attends to a Wellington Mk III at Hixon, one of a sizeable number of OTU bases at which crews were formed.

WELLINGTON Mk IV

The Wellington Mk IV was to prove unique among the many Wellington variants put into operational service in that it was powered by engines of non-British origin. Shortly after War was declared plans were made for installing American manufactured Pratt and Whitney Twin Wasp engines. However, it was not until the following February that the *neutral* United States government gave the necessary permission for the P&W Twin Wasp engine to be made available to Vickers — this came at a time when the Air Ministry was actively considering the abandonment of the project. However, an overall shortage of aero engines created a quick change of heart on the Air Ministry's part.

A Chester built Wellington IC (R1220) was selected as the test-bed for the 1050 hp R-1830-S3C4-C Twin Wasps engines, making its maiden flight from Chester in December of 1940. Hamilton Standard propellers were initially carried but because of their excessive noise they were soon replaced with Curtiss electric propellers. Despite an unfortunate crash-landing of the prototype at Weybridge during its landing approach, which was later traced to carburetor failure, several Wellington Mk IVs were forwarded to Boscombe Down for general testing. One ship among these test aircraft was equipped with Lindholme Air Sea Rescue gear.

Although succeeding the Mk III in development and service the Mk IV was essentially similar to the Mk 1C including the FN5 and FN10 two-gun turrets, although the FN5 turret was replaced on some aircraft by the FN20 four gun turret. The fuselage windows appear to have been blanked over on the few photographic examples of the Mark IV, however, beam gun windows were carried. Performance was essentially similar to the Mk III with the notable exception of top speed which was rated at 299 mph, some 44 mph than the Mk III.

Full scale production quickly began with squadron deliveries being made during August of 1941 to No 300, 301 (Polish), and No 458 (Australian) Squadrons, with No 142 and No 460 (Australian) Squadrons re-equipping in October and November respectively. A late-comer to Wellington Mk IV usage was 305 (Polish) Squadron in August of 1942. An unusual use of the Mk IV Wimpy was indulged in by No 544 (PR) Squadron, which operated a small number of specially equipped photographic reconnaissance Mk IVs on night photographic experiments over Britain. These experimental photo recon Wellingtons were replaced by Mosquitoes during early 1943.

While some engine starting problems were encountered, the aircraft provided good service to its six main squadrons. The two Australian squadrons relinquished their Mk IVs during 1942 as did 142 Squadron, while the three Polish Squadrons converted — or in the case of 301 Squadron disbanded — between January and May of 1943. In all, some 220 Wellington Mk IVs were built at the Chester plant.

(Above) The carburetor air intake atop the cowling is the sole indication that R1220 is the Pratt and Whitney powered Mk IV prototype and not a standard Mk 1C airframe.

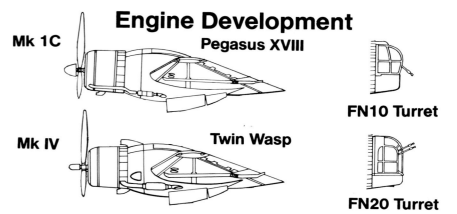

Engine Development

Mk 1C **Pegasus XVIII**

Mk IV **Twin Wasp**

FN10 Turret

FN20 Turret

(Right) This early Mk IV carries the original DeHavilland/Hamilton propellers whose high noise-output caused their prompt replacement with Curtiss props. R1515 crashed on take-off at Mullaghmore on 20 December 1943.

WELLINGTON MK V

A question constantly on the minds of both aircraft designers and the RAF Air Staff was how to go through the German air defenses without suffering prohibitive losses. And as the Kammhuber Line grew in length, depth and effectiveness it became increasingly obvious that the German defenses would have to be penetrated rather than circumvented. Bombers flying at the highest altitude would have the greatest chance of escaping the *Nachtjagd* (Nightfighters) and possibly the worst of the flak. Preliminary work on a high altitude Wellington had begun in 1938, with two Wellington prototypes — one equipped with Hercules engines and one with Merlin engines — being ordered in May of 1939. Pushed by the energetic Minister for Aircraft Production, Sir Max Aitken (Lord Beaverbrook), high altitude research efforts were redoubled after the Fall of France in June of 1940.

Development of the Hercules powered High altitude variant was pursued under the designation Wellington Mk V. Wellington 1C/R3298 was fitted with 1,425 hp Hercules III engines and Wellington IC/R3299 with 1,600 hp Hercules VIII engines. Also under consideration as a power source was the 1,425 hp Hercules XI utilizing GEC exhaust-driven turbo superchargers which were eventually retrofitted to R3299. Only one other Wellington Mk V was built, this being W5797. The twenty-eight airframes intended for Mk V production were converted to the Mk VI configuration.

The initial prototype, Wellington Mk V R3298, took to the air for the first time in September of 1940. The distinctive fuselage shape, the upper nose faired flush with the top surfaces of the fuselage and the lower nose with a definite shark-shaped contour, set a standard for subsequent high altitude aircraft. A crew of three was accommodated in a long cylindrical pressurized cabin built into the upper nose area. The pilot was provided with an eliptical bubble canopy slightly off-set to the port side and in line with the propellers. Cabin pressure was initially set at approximately 10,000 feet as opposed to the theoretical maximum operating height of 36,000 feet which was the anticipated operational altitude of the aircraft. Engines for production aircraft were to be turbo-supercharged.

Very high altitudes posed a number of unexpected problems even at the 30,000 feet which the Mk V reached. Icing-up of the canopy was a constant problem and was believed to be primarily due to cabin humidity. Grease solidifying in the control hinge bearings led to flying controls and trimmer circuits seizing up as well as adversely affecting the operation of the bomb-doors and rear turret. During one flight frozen lumps of oil from an engine leak were thrown against the fuselage by the propellers, resulting in heavy damage to the aircraft structure. One of the most serious problems was ice accumulation on the exterior skin which hindered the crew from opening the door during an emergency without first de-pressurizing the cabin — which took ten minutes! Prototypes W5797 and R3299, powered with Hercules VIII engines, experienced a similar range of problems to the Hercules III powered R3298. Externally the only difference was the shape of the canopy with the Hercules VIII powered aircraft having a circular shaped canopy.

When the Hercules engines did not live up to expectations development of the Mk V was terminated in favor of the Merlin powered Wellington Mk VI. However, work with the Wellington Mk V's pressurized cabin provided the basis upon which similar units were developed for the Spitfire and the Westland Welkin.

Developed in parallel with the Mk V the Wellington Mk VI was intended from the onset to use 1,600 hp Merlin 60 in-line oil cooled engines. The fuselage of the Mk VI prototype was essentially the same as the Mk V. However, the production Mk VI had a slightly lower nose section with a slightly steeper contour. The pilot's canopy was altered to a circular bubble with a DF loop enclosed in a clear perspex fairing located immediately behind the canopy.

While the original order placed with Vickers was for 132 high altitude Wellingtons spread between both the Mk V and Mk VI, actual production would be limited to sixty-seven machines, including the three Mk V prototypes. Of the sixty-four remaining aircraft twenty-eight were in fact Mk V airframes powered with Merlin 60 engines under the designation Wellington Mk VIA. The other thirty-two aircraft, substantive Mk VIs, carried the suffix G, these being either used as trainers for, or operators of, the blind target marking device code named *Oboe*.

(Above) The first Wellington Mk V prototype (R3298) had an elliptical cockpit canopy and the exhausts were located above the cowling face.

Wellington Mk VI prototypes (W5795 and W5800) carried a crew of four, with entry into the pressurized cabin being from the rear through the bomb-bay. These machines were equipped with additional wing sections increasing the wing-span by 12 feet allowing an altitude of 40,000 feet to be reached. Problems of ice accumulation, solidifying lubrication, heating and air-conditioning failures plagued most test flights of the Mk VI just as they had the Mk V.

High-altitude bombing tests were conducted with the Sperry bombsight, with the proposed FN70 turret being the sole defensive measure. The *Oboe* equipment carried by Wellington Mk VIGs provided extremely precise results for Bomber Command's Pathfinder Force, particularly when used as target markers from the winter of 1942/43 onwards. However, by this time the Mosquito had largely begun to take over the intended high altitude role of the Wellington Mk VIG. The Mosquito was able to deliver its bomb or target-marking load at an altitude very nearly the same as that of the Mk VIG, and its greater speed and maneuverability provided the *Wooden Wonder* with a much higher survival factor — and without the need for pressurized cabins!

Two aircraft, W5801 and W5802, were attached to No 109 Squadron for special radio experiments at Stradishall in March of 1942, with W5802 being transferred to RAE Farnborough during the following September. DR480 and DR484 were equipped with Type 423 gear which allowed the carriage of the 4,000 pound 'Cookie'. By 1943, however, the need for a high altitude Wimpy had come to an end, and some sixty were ignominiously scrapped at various maintenance units.

(Below) The second prototype (R3299) was marked with a Yellow 'P' and Yellow undersurfaces indicating its prototype status. It had a circular canopy and side-mounted exhausts. Only three Mk Vs were constructed before development was terminated in favor of the Mk VI.

(Above Left) DR484 is a Wellington Mk VI high-altitude bomber whose clear fuselage strip windows were superfluous since the crew was located in a sealed pressurized cabin within the forward nose section. The tail turret has been faired over. The under-surface color extends up the fuselage sides to the top of the side windows. This aircraft was one of the two High altitude Mk VIs equipped with 4,000 pound bomb-carrying gear known as Type 423.

(Above Right) The W5798 was an airframe originally built as a Mk V but its Hercules radials were replaced by Merlin 60s under the designation Wellington Mk VIA. The aircraft was the first of a batch of twenty-seven Mk V airframes modified to Mk VIA standards with Merlin inline engines intended for use as high altitude precision bombers. This aircraft was tested at RAE Farnborough using a Sperry bomb-sight.

Wellington Mk V and Mk VI

Mk V

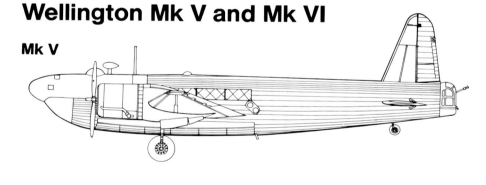

(Below) The Mk VIA W5796 looks extremely bulky when compared with the normal Wellington outline. The outline of the revised entry door can be seen running through the fuselage roundel. The Lorenz blind landing aerial has also been re-positioned.

Mk VI

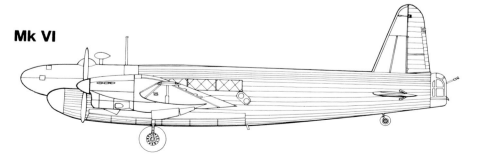

38

WELLINGTON MK X

With the 20/20 vision of hindsight the Wellington Mk X has been judged by most to be the high water mark of Wellington development, and it was no coincidence that production numbers totalled 3,803 aircraft — more than thirty percent of all Wellington production. The use of recently introduced light alloy parts which matched the strength but not the weight of standard mild steel components contributed greatly to a general performance increase of the Mk X over its predecessors. All up weight (AUW) was raised to 36,000 pounds, 2,500 pounds above the Mk III, and general performance was at least on a par with the Mk III in all categories except bomb load which was reduced from 4,500 to 4,000 pounds.

Powerplants were Hercules VIs or Hercules XVIs, with lengthened carburetor intakes on the cowlings and bell-shaped spinner fairings providing the essential external differences when compared to the the Mk III. Two Mk IIIs (X3374 and X3595) served as prototypes. Production was concentrated wholly at the Blackpool (1369) and Chester (2434) factories with Squadron deliveries commencing in late 1942. By March of 1943 twelve Squadrons of Bomber Command were either partially or fully equipped with the Mark X. However, during the course of 1943 Wellington Mk Xs were replaced by four-engined bombers in all twelve squadrons.

While its use as a firstline bomber in Europe was comparatively brief, the Mk X's deployment in the Middle East, Italy, and Burma ensured its continued importance as a strategic bomber. No 205 Group based in Italy's Foggia Plain, made up of No 37, 70 and 142 Squadrons, only relinquished the Wellington Mk X after September of 1944. In the Far East No 99 and 215 Squadrons soldiered on with their Mk Xs until August and September of 1944. Not only were the Wellingtons used to attack Japanese airfields and supply dumps, but during the critical Imphal battle of mid-1944 both units ferried bombs up to Hurri-bomber Squadrons operating from the Imphal Plain against the main Japanese supply arteries!

Those Wellingtons withdrawn from Bomber Command operations were transferred in large numbers to various OTUs. Indeed, Wellington Mk Xs were used as Post-War trainers under the designation Wellington T Mk 10 until March of 1953 when the last example (LP806) belonging to No 1 Air Navigation School was retired.

The Mk X was another Wellington variant favored by aero engine designers as a test-bed. A number were used to test the high altitude performance of the Hercules 38 while equipped with single GEC turbo-blowers. LN718 carried Hercules 100 engines which were intended for use in both the Halifax and the Wellington's Post-War civil airliner variant, the Viking. Noise tests conducted by Bristol involved RP484 with her engines incorporating the ability to be 'feathered' with presumably the reverse facility to 'un-feather' at the crucial moment! LN715 with its turrets faired over was a test-bed for the Rolls-Royce Dart turbo-prop which would be successfully used on the Vickers Viscount airliner.

(Above) A Wellington Mk X gracefully crests the clouds. The bell shaped spinners and the exhausts located on the inside of the engine cowlings are the main identification of the Hercules powered variant. The mass balances on the upper rudder can be seen silhouetted against the sky. The cockpit framing is unpainted metal. The White dots beneath the port wing are the twin landing lights, and the pitot mast can be seen below the starboard wing.

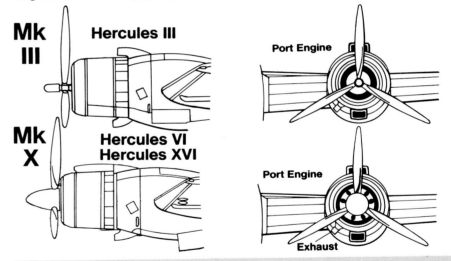

Mk III — Hercules III — Port Engine

Mk X — Hercules VI / Hercules XVI — Port Engine — Exhaust

(Right) This Mk X is seen at Glatton, the home of the US Eighth Air Force's 457th BG between 1944/45. The CO Code letters indicate that the aircraft belongs to an Operational Training Unit (OTU). The reason for its diversion to Glatton is unknown — possibly the crew had heard of the lavish cooking on USAAF bases!

(Above Left) On 22 February 1943 Major General James H Doolittle, the 'boss' of the North West African Strategic Air Force flew in 'A Apple' of No 150 Squadron from Blida during a raid on Bizerta's docks. The pilot was Flight Officer Roberts. Doolittle is the second from the left.

(Above Right) The aircraft's artwork is of J P Reilly Foul, a British newspaper cartoon character. A lucky horseshoe is fastened to the bomber's nose.

(Below Left) The inherent strength of the Wellington airframe was never better demonstrated than by this Mk X of 428 (Ghost) Squadron RCAF. NA:Y/HE239 was dealt a potentially lethal blow by flak over Duisburg on 8/9 April 1943. Sgt L F Williamson's successful efforts to bring home his crippled charge rightly earned him the Distinguished Conduct Medal.

(Below Right) Mine-laying operations under the code-name 'Gardening' were an important part of Bomber Command's mission. This Mk X is being raised with air-bags after a mine-laying sortie on 15 March 1943.

(Above Left) This Wellington Mk X (LP201), *Sister Anna*, was the specially adapted personal aircraft of AVM Keukny, the Director of Maintenance and Supply (Middle East and Central Mediterranean Forces). The starboard fuselage has a baggage hatch under the cockpit and an entrance door has been built into the fuselage side.

(Below Left) A line-up of Hercules powered Wellington Mk Xs belonging to No 426 (RCAF) Squadron during 1943 just prior to converting to Hercules powered Lancaster Mk IIs. This close parking of bombers seems to indicate the RAF's relative immunity from attacks by the *Luftwaffe*.

(Above Right) *Sister Anna* carries no spinner fairings and is painted in the Coastal Command color scheme. Keukny's rank pennant beneath the cockpit was painted on both sides of the nose and the nose turret was faired over. Among the crew is W/O J Wade the WOP/AG.

(Below Right) An interesting variety of Allied aircraft at Blida in North Africa during 1943. Two Bostons stand to the right while a P51A is seen head-on in the center, and four Hurricanes skim low across the field, possibly returning from a sortie. A solitary Mk X Wimpy crouches on the left.

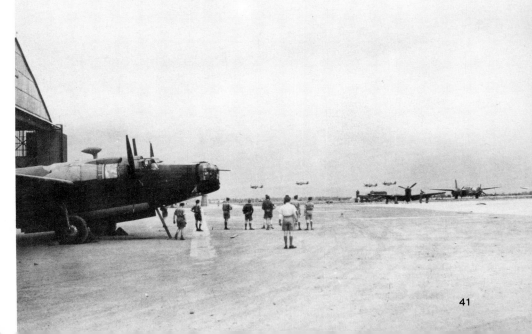

Mk Xs taxi out for a twilight take-off. The stark simplicity of this scene effectively captures the spirit and reality of Bomber Command operations as dusk gave way to the cloak of darkness under which Germany's industrial resources were hammered to destruction.

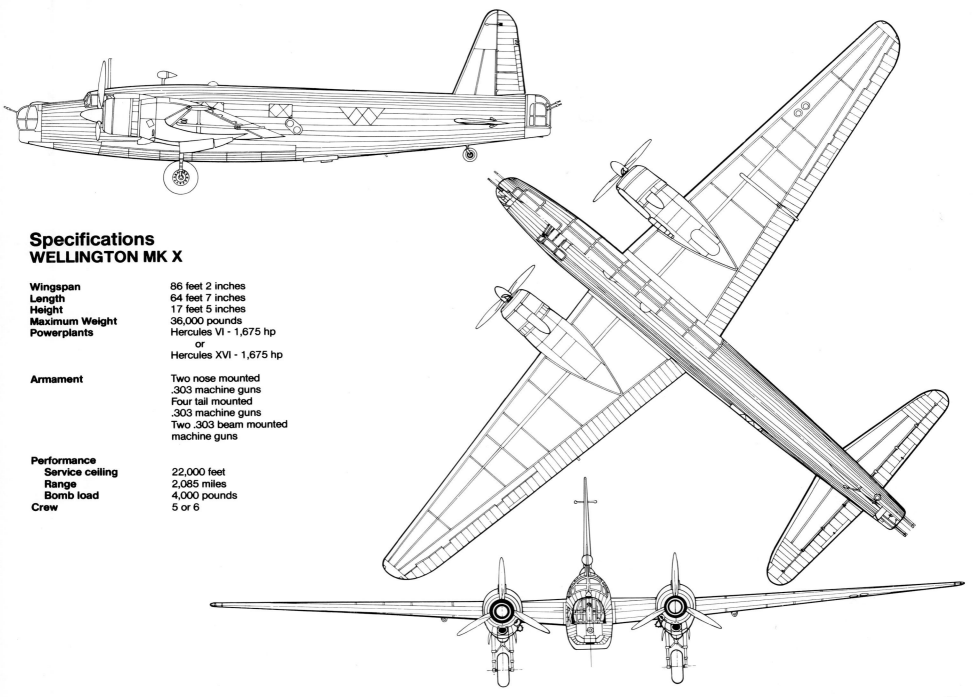

Specifications
WELLINGTON MK X

Wingspan	86 feet 2 inches
Length	64 feet 7 inches
Height	17 feet 5 inches
Maximum Weight	36,000 pounds
Powerplants	Hercules VI - 1,675 hp
	or
	Hercules XVI - 1,675 hp
Armament	Two nose mounted
	.303 machine guns
	Four tail mounted
	.303 machine guns
	Two .303 beam mounted
	machine guns
Performance	
Service ceiling	22,000 feet
Range	2,085 miles
Bomb load	4,000 pounds
Crew	5 or 6

WELLINGTON MK XI

Coastal Command's generally favorable experiences with the Wellington GR Mk VIII both as a torpedo bomber and in the anti-submarine role encouraged the RAF to work with Vickers in producing up-dated versions of the Wellington specifically to carry out Coastal Command missions. What was to prove to be the first of a quartet of purpose-built Wellington variants developed for Coastal Command was adapted from the standard Mk X airframe. Under the designation Wellington GR Mk XI, the torpedo bomber was equipped with ASV Mk II radar (Type 454) that featured a row of four large external aerials mounted along the fuselage spine and two rows of four 'T' aerials mounted along each rear fuselage side. Otherwise, externally the Wellington GR Mk VIII was essentially similar to its Mk X predecessor. Provision was also made for carrying the later ASV Mk III radar which required a re-design of the aircraft's nose. However, the ASV III radar would become more of a standard feature on the later GR Mk XII and GR Mk XIV.

Since German merchant vessels were now sailing in heavily protected convoys which included merchantmen modified as flak ships, forward fire-power was becoming increasingly important for torpedo bombers. 180 GR Mk XI airframes were constructed between the Weybridge (105) and Blackpool (75) factories.

Although the Mk XI was employed primarily in Coastal Command the camouflage scheme seen on many GR Mk XIs was not the low-visibility Greys over White normally associated with Coastal Command, but rather the Dark Earth and Green over Black scheme of Bomber Command. Certainly the latter color scheme afforded as much if not greater concealment from enemy observation when carrying out the low-level stalking of merchant convoys.

WELLINGTON MK XII
Anti Submarine

The second GR aircraft developed from the Mk X airframe was the Wellington GR Mk XII an anti-submarine Wellington fitted with ASV Mk III radar which had first been installed in some GR Mk XIs. The ASV Mk III radar was not dependent on external aerials, the radar gear being carried in a nose-mounted 'Tear-drop' fairing with the FN5 nose turret being removed and replaced by a clear nose canopy similar to the perspex units carried on early Mk Is.

However, some form of forward fire-power was now becoming essential when engaging U-Boats, since by 1943, when the GR Wimpys were coming into full service, U-boats were carrying additional armor plating and bristling with anti-aircraft guns and had adopted a policy of remaining on the surface and fighting it out with attacking Allied patrol aircraft. A pair of flexible Browning machine guns were located in the lower part of the canopy with which to engage U-boat flak gunners during the attack-run using the belly mounted Leigh Light beam to sight by.

Fifty-eight GR Mk XIIs were produced with Weybridge again being the majority producer (50) and Blackpool turning out eight. In common with the GR Mk XI, the GR Mk XII was committed to action during the course of 1943. The U-boat tactic of remaining on the surface and slugging it out with Allied aircraft inevitably resulted in the loss of some Wellingtons when during one-to-one fights. One remedy for this was for an aircraft to shadow the U-boat while calling up support. When help arrived a co-ordinated attack could then be carried out. Even more lethal to German submarines was the introduction of the Mk 24 'homing' torpedo for use after the U-boat had submerged! Between these various measures the anti-submarine forces compelled the enemy to revert to a policy of evasion by either crash-diving — a self-defeating tactic when 'homing' torpedoes were part of the attacker's weaponry — or remaining submerged.

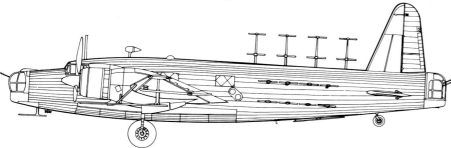

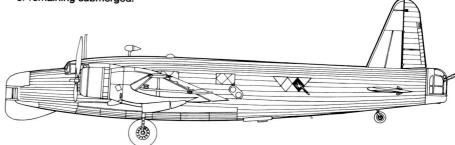

(Below Left) 'S Sugar' of No 304 (Polish) Squadron, a Wellington Mk XI but is not equipped with the ASV Mk II radar aerials. The upper camouflage colors are the Brown and Green of Bomber Command instead of the Grey/Green combination normally carried over White lower surfaces on Coastal Command aircraft. The fuselage windows appear to be absent.

(Below Right) Ignominiously dragged to an area more resembling a pasture than an airfield this Mk XII awaits the salvage yard in the company of a Wimpy from a Bomber Command. Neither aircraft can be identified with a particular Squadron. The reason for the 'X' markings on the Mk XII is unknown.

WELLINGTON GR MK XIII

A further development of the Mk X airframe for the daylight torpedo bomber the Wellington GR Mk XIII was equipped with externally mounted ASV Mk II radar, and powered by a pair of 1,735 hp Hercules XVII engines, the highest rated engines to power the Wellington. Production was 844 aircraft with 842 being produced at Blackpool with only two being built at at Weybridge.

These aircraft were operated in both the European and Mediterranean Theater of Operations with numbers of the former to be seen wearing Bomber Command colors rather than those of Coastal Command.

After the war eight were sold to Greece.

(Above Right) The Empire Air Navigation School (E.A.N.S.) employed a variety of aircraft which included this Wellington GR Mk XIII. The guns have been removed from the rear turret and a diamond pattern window has been installed in the fuselage side. Lindholme 1947.

WELLINGTON GR MK XIV

The Wellington GR Mk XIV was an anti-submarine Wimpy carrying nose mounted ASV Mk III centimetric radar and a Leigh Light. To install the radar the nose turret was removed, however, some machines had the outline of a turret painted on to disguise the fact that they were unarmed at the nose. Similar to the GR Mk XIII, the GR Mk XIV was also powered by the 1,735 hp Hercules engine. Production was 841 with machines being built at all three plants, Chester (538), Weybridge (53), and Blackpool (230).

Large numbers of Mk XIVs flew missions from Bomber Command airfields along the South Coast of England during the weeks before and after the 6 June 1944 Invasion of France and went a long way in thwarting efforts by German U-boats to penetrate the vast convoys moving men and material across the English Channel. Upwards of ten enemy U-Boats were sent to the bottom of the narrow channel. At least one was sunk by a Wellington Mk XIV of No 304 Squadron, and doubtless many more were diverted from their task by the relentless presence of the GR Wimpy.

Following the end of the War Wellington GR Mk XIVs were sold to France, who employed them in the same role as Coastal Command, though in a much more peaceful scenario.

(Above) This Wellington GR Mk XIII presents a sad sight after crash-landing in Nigeria. Its ASV Mk II aerials denotes its anti-submarine role. It has a variation in the fuselage window layout with a division between the forward and center sections. The gaping cockpit hatches suggest a hasty evacuation of the aircraft crew.

(Below) A bustling scene at the Brooklands Aviation repair center at Sywell in 1945. The nearest aircraft is ME898 belonging to No 6 (C) OTU carrying ASV Mk II aerials. The aircraft alongside is probably a Bomber Command Mk X formerly of No 8 OTU.

(Below) The size of the ASV Mk III Radar cover under the nose, can be seen silhouetted against the ground. The nose canopy bears a strong similarity to that fitted on the Wellington Mk I.

(Below Right) These Mk XIVs belong to No 304 (Polish) Squadron engaged in anti-submarine duties. Those in the background all sport an extra DF loop fairing ahead and below the standard fitting.

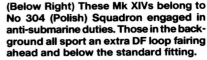

45

WELLINGTON C MK XV
WELLINGTON C Mk XVI

Until the latter days of the Second World War the RAF was woefully deficient in transport aircraft. One of the temporary remedies again involved the Wellington. Selected Mk 1As and Mk 1Cs were converted by Vickers into transport aircraft. Because they varied considerably, details of internal changes are unclear, but the main external modifications lay in removal of both nose and tail turrets, reappearance of the fuselage window strips, and installation of a starboard side fuselage door midway between the main wing and tailplane. The absence of defensive weapons was disguised on some aircraft by the painting of turret frame lines to create the illusion of turrets. These Wellington transports were initially designated Wellington C Mk 1A and C Mk 1C, however they were subsequently redesignated to Wellington C Mk XV and C Mk XVI. The exact number of Wimpys converted to the transport role is unknown, but their presence in the various Theaters of War was of great benefit, given the relative shortage of purpose-built transport aircraft.

C Mk XV (Mk 1A)

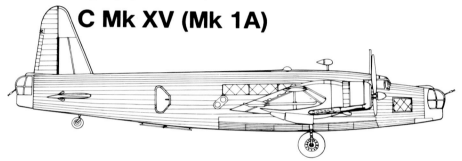

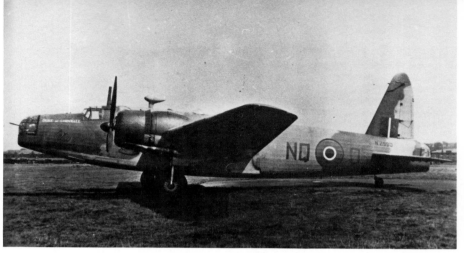

(Above) Formerly a Mk 1A, NQ D/N2990 was converted to Mk XV transport standards bearing the title *DUKE of CORNWALL*. Outlines of turrets have been painted on the nose and tail. The color scheme is believed to be Brown and Green over Grey undersurfaces. The aircraft belongs to No 24 Squadron and is seen at RAF Hendon sometime during 1943.

(Below) This C Mk XV (NQ A), sister aircraft of NQ D, carries *DUKE of RUTLAND* on the nose. The nose and tail fairings have been slimmed-down and extended. The fuselage window strip has also been extended to a point just ahead of the C1 fuselage roundel.

This C Mk XVI (Mk 1C) transport variant is similar in configuration to the No 24 Squadron Mk XV, with the exception of the turret fairings which in this case carry no false frame-lines. Twin diamond markings behind the fuselage door are believed to be first-aid kits which were sewn into the fabric.

WELLINGTON TRAINERS

Wellington T Mk XVII

This crew trainer Wellington variant was based on the conversion of a Mk XI under the designation Wellington T Mk XVII intended for training nightfighter crews. It carried a Mosquito type bulbous nose covering an SCR720 Airborne Intercept radar set replacing the FN5 nose turret. The rear turret was removed and faired over.

Wellington T Mk XVIII

Externally similar to the T Mk XVII the Wellington T Mk XVIII was internally fitted with radar and wireless equipment with which to train radio operators and navigators. Eighty aircraft were completed under this designation at Blackpool.

Wellington T Mk XIX

In contrast the last of the trainer trio was a service conversion of the Mk X which fulfilled the duties of a basic Wellington bomber crew trainer. While the T Mk XVI and the T Mk XVIIs used Hercules XVII engines the Wellington T Mk XIX bomber trainers were powered by both Hercules XVIs and XVIIs engines.

(Below) Seen at a Public Air Show during the late Forties or early Fifties, LP597 of No 5 Air Navigation School is liberally equipped with aerials on the fuselage spine. Reversion to the continuous fuselage window strip was a feature of the T Mk 10 as was the retention of the rear turret, although minus guns.

(Above) A Wellington T Mk 10 of No 1 Air Navigation School at its Topcliffe, Yorks base in 1948/49. An overall Silver finish with Yellow trainer bands around the rear fuselage and central wing areas now replaces the drab but necessary colors of War.

(Above Left) NC892 of an un-identified training unit reveals how the nose turrets on T10s were faired over. The aerials on the side of the nose just ahead and below the cockpit are part of the Rebecca landing approach system.

(Above Right) The sole intact example of the Wimpy, at least until a Mk 1A was dragged out of Loch Ness during the autumn of 1985, is displayed at Abingdon on 14 June 1968. Although the aircraft is a T10, she was displayed in Bomber Command colors to depict the Wellington's primary function as a wartime bomber.

RP413 is a T Mk XVIII Wireless and Navigator trainer, her status as a trainer is indicated by the Yellow fuselage band. The bulbous cover for the SCR720 AI radar prominently stands out on the nose. The distinctive post-war roundel and fin flashes are carried.

(Above) Lengthened fuselage and wingspan denote this aircraft as a Warwick, a parallel-design to the Wellington powered by the slim shaped Twin Wasp engines. HF947 belongs to No 280 Squadron, operating in the ASR role in the Far East just after the War's end. The ASV aerials can be seen under the wing along with the return to the pre-War practice of carrying under-wing serial numbers. *SNAKE* painted below the serial number on the rear fuselage was common to many Far East Theater aircraft at the end of the War. Type C roundels are carried under the wings.

(Below) The transport Warwick CIII (HG338) of No 304 Squadron has a new streamlined nose, faired over tail turret, and a detachable cargo pannier slung into position on the belly. The open personnel door at the rear of the fuselage seems to be part of a larger cargo door. South East Asia Command (SEAC) markings in two-tone Blue are carried.